PRE-GED
WRITING SKILLS

REVISED

GLENCOE
McGraw-Hill

New York, New York   Columbus, Ohio   Mission Hills, California   Peoria, Illinois

GED • GED • GED • GED • GED

Acknowledgments
Unless otherwise indicated, all photographs are the property of Glencoe Publishing Co.

Cover Photo: Aaron Haupt

Imprint 1996

Send all inquiries to:
Glencoe/McGraw-Hill
936 Eastwind Drive
Westerville, OH 43081

ISBN 0-02-802069-3

4 5 6 7 8 9 10 11 12   DBH   02 01 00 99 98 97 96

Glencoe Pre-GED Program
Consultants to the Program

Jeff Bishop
New Brunswick Adult Learning Center
New Brunswick, NJ

Kathryn Boesel-Dunn
Columbus Public Schools
Columbus, Ohio

Toby G. Cannon
Cohn Adult Learning Center
Nashville, Tennessee

Charmaine M. Carney
Hawkeye Institute of Technology
Waterloo, Iowa

Mary S. Charuhas
College of Lake County
Grayslake, Illinois

Lee Chic
Sequoia Adult School
Redwood City, California

James R. Fryxell
College of Lake County
Grayslake, Illinois

Marcia Harrington
D.C. Public Library
Washington, D.C.

Cynthia A. Green
Lincoln Instructional Center
Dallas, Texas

Esther Gross
Petit Jean Technical College
Morrilton, Arkansas

Theodore M. Harig
Ellsworth Correctional Center
Union Grove, Wisconsin

Chuck Herring
GED Institute
Seattle, Washington

Linda L. Kindy
Little Rock Adult Education Center
Little Rock, Arkansas

Claudia V. McClain
South Suburban College
South Holland, Illinois

Ed A. Mayfield
Fayette County Adult Education
Center
Lexington, Kentucky

Valerie Meyer
Southern Illinois University
Edwardsville, Illinois

Pat Mitchell
Dallas Independent School District
Dallas, Texas

Laura Morris
Center for Community Education
Tallahassee, Florida

Evelyn H. Nunes
Virginia Commonwealth University
Richmond, Virginia

Jill Plaza
Reading and Educational Consultants
Palatine, Illinois

John H. Redd
Dallas Independent School District.
Dallas, Texas

Gail Rice
Adult Basic Education Program
Palos Heights, Illinois

Karen Samson
Chicago State University
Chicago, Illinois

Yvonne E. Siats-Fiskum
Gateway Technical College
Elkhorn, Wisconsin

Sheldon Silver
Truman College
Chicago, Illinois

Robert T. Sutton
Central Piedmont Community College
Charlotte, North Carolina

Dee Swanson
Minnesota Correctional Facility
Stillwater, Minnesota

Ann Kuykendall Parker
Cohn Adult Learning Center
Nashville, Tennessee

Contents

Part B
Writing Paragraphs / 107

How to Use This Book

How do you feel about writing? Here's what some people say:

"I just can't write."

"There are too many rules!"

"I never learned how."

Do you ever feel the same way? If so, you can relax. *Glencoe Pre-GED Writing Skills* has been written for you. Step by step, this book will teach you the basic rules for good writing.

You won't simply learn the rules. You'll have many chances to practice them. You'll write sentences and paragraphs on many different topics. You'll learn to find your mistakes and correct them.

This book is divided into two parts. In **Part A,** you'll learn **word skills** and **sentence skills.** You'll practice writing different kinds of sentences.

In **Part B,** you'll use your sentence-writing skills to create **paragraphs.** You'll learn how to get ideas for writing. You'll practice writing different kinds of paragraphs.

Measuring What You Know

Each part of this book begins with a survey of what you already know about writing. Don't worry if you can't answer every question — this book will teach you the skills you don't know.

The Lessons

Most of the lessons start with a picture. The picture will help you get started with the lesson. That's why this section is called **Picture It.**

The next part of each lesson, **Here's an Example,** gives you an example of the skills taught in the lesson. In **Working It Out** you'll practice these skills by doing some exercises.

A **Writing on Your Own** section gives you a chance to do your own writing. And finally, the **Looking Back** section sums up the lesson's main idea.

Measuring What You've Learned

Each part of the book ends with a **test.** The test measures how much you've learned. It also helps you see what you need to review.

Answers

All the answers in the book are explained in the **Answers** section at the back of the book.

Writing Skills

Part A
Writing Words and Sentences

In **Part A,** you will begin to build skills in writing. The lessons give you a chance to write words that speak for you. In the process, you'll find that your written vocabulary will increase. Your words will become stronger and more effective.

You will also practice writing your ideas in sentences. You'll expand your sentences with words that describe. You'll use writing to help you as you read about or listen to new ideas. You'll learn how to catch and correct mistakes in your sentences.

As you write, your skill at writing will improve. You'll find it easier to learn to write paragraphs. Better than that, you'll find that writing is useful — at your job, with your family and friends, and in your free time. Writing well is a skill you will be able to use for life.

Measuring What You Know

This book will help you write well. You can test your writing skills on this short survey. The survey will show you what you already know. Don't worry if you don't know all the answers— this book will teach you what you don't know!

A. Complete the following sentences. Write a word from the box in each blank.

There are _____ ways to be a good cook. For
                    1

example, some people refuse to follow a _____ .
                                        2

They like to _____ at what to add next. These cooks
              3

are interesting because they never _____ a meal!
                                    4

guess	repeat
several	recipe

B. Underline the correct verb in each sentence.
5. Barry (has/have) some strange ideas.
6. We (go/went) to Maryville last weekend.
7. The girls (wants/want) bicycles for Christmas.
8. I (am/be) tired of cleaning all the time.
9. You (was/were) wrong about Rick.

C. Each of the following sentences is in the present verb time. Rewrite them in the past verb time.

10. Tony goes to the gym for a workout.

_____

11. The Carsons walk a mile to the store.

_____

12. I do pushups twice a day.

_____

D. Compare these two sentences:

- The cat climbed the tree.
  The fearless cat climbed swiftly
  to the top of the old pine tree.

*Both sentences are correct. But the second sentence gives more **descriptive details**. Rewrite the following sentences with* *descriptive details.*

13. The storm passed over the town.

_____

14. Jackie read in the library.

_____

E. Correct each of the following sentences. Cross out the mistakes and write the corrections above them. There are two mistakes in each sentence.

15. One never knows if you will win or loose.

16. Each Kitten has a white spot on their nose.

17. Judge Ramirez told raymond to tell the Truth.

18. Its easy too learn how to drive.

19. Stephanie will chose a new partner in september.

20. This stew has to much garlic in them.

21. The grabowskis are putting a pool in they're yard.

22. During Summer, I swim every thursday.

F. The following sentences contain a number of errors. Rewrite each sentence correctly in the lines below. Add words if necessary.

23. we were glad to relax after a long day

_____

24. The baby monkey, quick and alert.

_____

G. Write a sentence about your favorite food.

25. _____

H. Write a question about one of your hobbies.

26. _____

I. Combine the details in the following sentence pairs to make one sentence.

27. One day Marcia felt sad. It was a cold, rainy day.

_____

28. We went to a movie last night. We went with Casey.

_____

29. Jeff sang at the concert. He sang like a rock-and-roll star.

_____

30. Dolphins swim quickly. They swim very gracefully.

_____

*J. Make one sentence from each of these sentence pairs. Combine either the **subjects** or the **verbs**.*

31. Darlene likes to travel. Dave likes to travel.

_____

32. Mike works during the day. He studies at night.

_____

K. Combine the following sentence pairs into one sentence. Use the words in parentheses. Watch your punctuation.

33. The player slid into home. The umpire called an out. (but)

_____

34. We shopped for groceries. We made dinner. (after)

_____

35. The wash had dried. I took it off the line. (so)

_____

36. Hans will finish on Thursday. He won't work on Friday. (since)

_____

L. Write a one-sentence summary of the following paragraph.

■ What does the word *secretary* mean to you? Do you picture a woman writing on a notepad while her male boss dictates a letter? If so, you have some catching up to do! For today's secretaries, computer skills are more important than dictation skills. Also, a secretary today probably works for a group of people, men and women. She — or he — has many new jobs to do. In fact, most secretaries are too busy to make coffee anymore!

37. _____

You can check your answers on page 237.

Using the Results

How did you do on the survey? Did you have problems with some of the questions? If you did, find those questions on the table below. You'll see which skills you need to practice more. You'll also see which lessons teach those skills.

Of course, you will want to work through every lesson in this book. This will strengthen the skills you already have. With practice, your writing skills will improve. The lessons in this book will make all your writing easier.

If you missed questions:	See lessons:	To learn these skills:
1, 2, 3, 4	5	context clues
5, 6, 7, 8, 9	11, 12	matching subjects and verbs
		verb times
10, 11, 12	12	verb times
13, 14	8, 18	adding details
15, 16, 17, 18, 19, 20, 21, 22	9, 10, 26	capitalization
		pronoun agreement
		using contractions and possessives
23, 24	14, 16	beginning capitalization
		end punctuation
		writing in complete sentences
25, 26	15, 16	writing in complete sentences
27, 28, 29, 30	18, 19	adding descriptive details
31, 32	20	combining subjects and verbs
33, 34, 35, 36	21, 22	combining complete thoughts
		combining unequal ideas
37	25	summarizing

Starting to Write

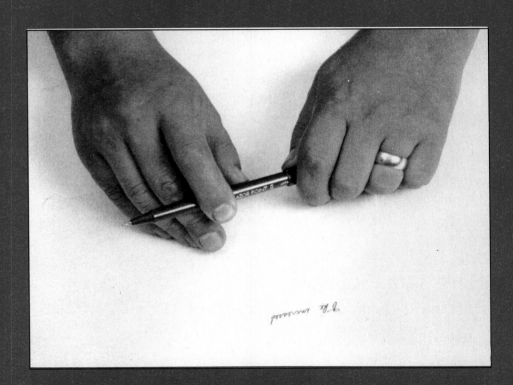

Speaking and Writing

In this lesson you will
- look at the differences between speaking and writing
- recognize formal and informal writing
- think about why you write and who will read your writing

Picture It

Look at the cartoon. What do you think the mother is saying to her son? What is the son saying to his mother? Write in a few words of conversation for each of them.

You can guess what the mother and son are saying by looking at their faces and their bodies. When someone talks to you, you can see if he or she is smiling or frowning. You can usually tell if he or she is nervous or relaxed, joking or serious. But with writing, you see only one thing — words.

That's why *writing* is different from *speaking*. With writing, you see only the words — and the words have to give the whole message.

Here's an Example

Read the following conversation between Judy and Florence.

Judy: "Bad day?"
Florence: "Yeah."
Judy: "How come? Your boss again?"
Florence: "No kidding. Crazy as ever."
Judy: "You'd better stay away from him."

Can you tell what Judy and Florence are talking about? They are talking about Florence's hard day at work, and about her "crazy" boss.

Now, suppose Florence wanted to write about her day. Which of these paragraphs gives more information?

Bad day. My crazy boss. So tired—sleeping at work.	I had a bad day today. My boss kept giving me more work. I was so tired I was falling asleep on the job.

The first paragraph is written the way Florence might say it out loud. It is **informal.** It doesn't give much information. You might ask: Who had a bad day? When? Who was tired?

The second paragraph gives more information. It is written in a more **formal** style. It is clear that *Florence* had a bad day *today* and almost fell asleep at work.

Working It Out

Read each pair of sentences. Put a ☑ next to the sentence that is more formal and gives more complete information.

1. **a.** Love the smell of that stuff. ☐
   b. I love the smell of fresh-baked bread. ☐
2. **a.** No way will Jeff's car run well now. ☐
   b. Since the accident, Jeff's car doesn't run well. ☐
3. **a.** Patty shouldn't tell me what to do. ☐
   b. Patty's got no right to butt in. ☐

Now let's look at some of the reasons *why* people write.

Here are some things Antonio wrote in one day. On the lines below each example, answer these questions. Whom was this written for? Why was it written? One is done for you.

1. For whom? *Antonio's neighbors*
   Why? *To tell them about the garage sale*

2. For whom? _____
   Why? _____

Garcia TV Repair
1050 S. Lincoln, Pine Lake

Billed to: *Jim O'Connor*

Date	Service	Amount
5/16	Repaired TV	$75

*Dear Lupe—
How are you? Are you still coming to see us next month? I hope so. Give me a call to let me know your plans.
See you soon—
Antonio*

3. For whom? _____

Why? _____

4. For whom? _____

Why? _____

When you write for yourself, you are the only one who needs to understand it. But when you write for other people, you need to be sure you've given them enough information.

➤ *Writing On Your Own*

Imagine that you have been feeling sick. You go to the doctor. The doctor asks you to write down your **symptoms,** so she knows what you're feeling. You write your symptoms on the form given below.

Fill in the missing words to complete the medical form.

_____   Dr. Lim
(Patient's Name)

_____
(Date)

Symptoms: I started feeling sick on _____

At first my throat felt _____ and I had a

fever. After a day, I began _____

and that was when I decided to see a doctor. Right now I feel

_____ and my throat _____ .

▲ Looking Back

Every time you write, ask yourself two questions:
- Who will read this?
- Why will they read it?

The answers to these questions will help you decide *what* information you need to include.

Knowing the Topic

> *In this lesson you will*
> - identify *what* a sentence is about (the topic)
> - write sentences on a topic

Picture It

In Lesson 1, you learned the differences between speaking and writing, and informal and formal writing. You thought about *why* you write and *who* will read your writing. Now you need to think about *what* you'll write. Every piece of writing has a **topic,** something that it is about.

What are Tom and Sandra talking about?

Tom: "Cammy was really surprised."
Sandra: "What did she do?"
Tom: "Oh, first she screamed. Then she started laughing. And then she tried to hug everyone at once."
Sandra: "I bet she'll never have another birthday like that one."

Did you guess? They are talking about Cammy's surprise birthday party. The party is the **topic** of their conversation.

Here's an Example

Conversations often jump from topic to topic. In the following conversation, Frank and Eddie discuss four topics. Write each topic in the correct space. An example is done for you.

> Frank: Boy, that was some great basketball last night. Eddie, did you see the game?

Topic: *basketball game*

1. Eddie: I sure didn't. Donna wasn't feeling well, so I took the kids to a movie. She had a bad cold all week.

Topic: _____

2. Frank: I had a cold last week. Missed two days of work and I'm still catching up. We're busy with spring orders now.

Topic: _____

3. Eddie: We're busy, too. I'm just hoping I can take a few days' vacation to get the garden in.

Topic: _____

Working It Out

Imagine walking into a television store. Every television is tuned to a different channel. On one TV screen, people are talking. On another they're singing or playing football—it gets confusing, doesn't it? It's much easier to watch one show at a time.

The same thing is true for writing. Your writing is clearer if you stick to one **topic** at a time.

Read each paragraph below. Circle the word that describes the topic of the paragraph. If you cannot tell what the topic is, circle ''not clear.''

1. Sometimes the sail of a boat is too tall to pass under the drawbridge. When this is so, the captain blows his boat horn. Then the bridge keeper pulls a lever to raise the bridge. Once the boat has passed under, the bridge keeper lowers the bridge again.

The topic of this paragraph is:

      boats   the ocean   a drawbridge   not clear

2. I like chocolate. My sister has been on a diet for twelve years. Supermarkets are very crowded on Saturdays. In the summertime, many people buy fresh fruit.

The topic of this paragraph is:

      chocolate   dieting   supermarkets   not clear

3. Many parents worry about violence on television. They don't want their children to see shows where people are killed or beaten up. They are afraid that their children will think it's all right to hurt people.

The topic of this paragraph is:

 hurting people   violence on TV   new TV shows   not clear

4. Dogs can be trained to obey many commands. It's hard to find an apartment if you have pets. When someone says, ''It's raining cats and dogs,'' they mean that it's raining hard.

The topic of this paragraph is:

dogs   rain   apartment-hunting   not clear

Writing On Your Own

Susan and Bill Walker are at home fixing supper. Part of their conversation is written below. Fill in the blanks to complete the conversation.

Susan: Lisa is late again, Bill. I told her to be home by 5:30.

Bill: Did you call the school? Maybe she _____ .
Susan: I called, but there's no answer. I'm really worried.
Bill: Did you call Tisha's mother? Maybe Lisa and Tisha

_____ .

Susan: Their line is busy.
Bill: Did you drive past the video arcade? Maybe she

_____ .

Susan: She'd better not have. I've told her over and over that

_____

What is the topic of this conversation? _____

Look at the following topics. Choose one of them. Write two sentences about that topic in the lines below.

Topics: car repair   voting   church   parades

_____

_____

_____

_____

▲ Looking Back

Before you write, decide *what* you're writing about, *who* will read it, and *why* they'll read it. Once you do that, you're on your way to becoming a good writer!

Practicing Your Penmanship

> *In this lesson you will*
> ■ practice writing in a clear, legible style

Picture It

Suppose you received the letter on the right. How would you answer it? Maybe it says that you won a million dollars. Maybe it says that a close friend is coming to town. Maybe the person is begging you to answer right away. But if you can't read someone's handwriting, you can't get the message!

So far in this book you've read about *why* you write, *whom* you write for, and *what* you write about. Let's think for a moment about *how* you write.

How is *your* handwriting? Here is a short quiz to help you decide if you need to work on your **penmanship**—in other words, your **handwriting.**

	Always	Sometimes	Never
I can easily read my handwriting.	____	____	____
My friends and family can easily read my handwriting.	____	____	____
My boss and/or teacher can easily read my handwriting.	____	____	____
I can fill out forms that say ''please print.''	____	____	____
I can fill out computer forms with boxes for each letter.	____	____	____

If you marked "Always" for every statement, you might not need to do this lesson. But if you marked "Sometimes" for some statements, you could probably use a little penmanship practice. And if you marked "Never" for *any* statement, you should definitely work on your handwriting before taking the GED Test.

Here's an Example

Everyone's handwriting is different. How boring it would be if everyone wrote the same way! But most handwriting falls into two types: **cursive writing** (connected letters) and **printing** (separate letters).

■ Box A is an example of **cursive writing.** Cursive writing is usually used for writing letters, essays, and other long pieces of writing.

■ Box B is an example of **printing.** Printing is often required on job applications, registration forms, and forms that will be read by computers.

It's a good idea to know both cursive writing and printing.

Box A

> *I am returning the stereo I bought from you because it does not work. I bought it only two weeks ago and the tape player has already stopped playing tapes.*

Box B

> I went to Washington High School for two years. My job experience includes three years as a waitress at Carney's Corner in Maplewood. I also worked in a day care center for one year.

Working It Out

Copy the following sentences twice. The first time, use cursive (connected) writing. The second time, print the sentences.

I am interested in working for Springcrest Hospital because I am a people-person. I like to help others, and I think sick people deserve good care.

_____

_____

_____

_____

_____

_____

When filling out computer forms, every letter and number should be very clear. Fill out the following form.

Last Name   First Name   Initial
(Please Print)

Month   Day   Year
Date of Birth

Home Address—Number and Street

Telephone

City   State   Zip Code

Are your numbers clear and readable?

What you write *with* can be important too. Find a pen that writes smoothly, without running or skipping. Use blue or black ink. If you use a felt-tip pen, be sure the tip is fine enough to keep the letters from running together.

When you write, you should usually use a pen instead of a pencil. However, sometimes you *must* use pencil—for example, when you are filling out a computer form like the one above. When you use a pencil, be sure the tip is sharp. If you erase something, erase it completely. Don't leave streaks or tear the paper.

Writing On Your Own

A good way to work on your handwriting is to keep a **journal** and write in it every day.

A **journal** is your private book—a notebook where you can write anything you like. You can write about your feelings, your life, and your ideas. This book will give you some ideas on things to write in your journal. Here's the first one: when you find a poem, a joke, or a quotation that you like, copy it down carefully in your journal. It's good practice!

Copy the following sentences twice—first in your best cursive writing, and then in printing. When you finish, look at the checklist given below. Can you answer "yes" to every question? If not, you need more practice.

- When you are looking for a job, good handwriting is important. After all, your job application is probably the first contact you'll have with the boss. If you want to make a good impression, good penmanship is the place to start!

_____

_____

_____

_____

_____

_____

_____

_____

	Yes	No
- Does my pen or pencil write clearly and smoothly, without smearing or skipping?	_____	_____
- Are my letters and numbers even and clear?	_____	_____
- Can I tell where words begin and end, and where sentences begin and end?	_____	_____
- Are my **punctuation marks**—commas, periods, exclamation points, and so on—easy to see?	_____	_____
- Do my letters have an even slant?	_____	_____

You can use this checklist each time you want to check your penmanship.

▲ Looking Back

Almost everything you write is read by someone else. If you want that person to understand your words, practice your handwriting! Remember to use the checklist to make sure you are getting your message across.

Free Writing

In this lesson you will
■ learn to "warm up" for writing by writing freely

Picture It

Good athletes make everything they do look easy. Good writing looks easy, too. But athletes know they have to warm up before they start—and so do writers!

One of the ways you can "warm up" for writing is by **free writing**—writing down everything that comes into your head for a set time. Sometimes you may have a particular topic. Or you can just start writing to see what happens. Many writers say their best ideas come when they are free writing.

When you free write, remember these points:

■ Decide how long you will write—for one minute, for ten minutes, until you fill half a page, or one full page. It's up to you.

■ Don't worry about spelling, grammar, or punctuation.

■ Don't stop writing until you reach the limit you set. If you run out of ideas, write the same word over and over until a new thought comes.

Here's an Example

This is what one writer wrote in one minute on food.

Food. Food. When I think of food I think of fruit which I like very much. I like apples we used to pick them off the trees when I was little. Also oranges. My favorite fruit is probably strawberries never eat too many I like them with cream, a little sugar.

An Idea to Remember
There's only one rule for free writing—KEEP WRITING!

Here's another way to practice free writing. Next to each word given below, write the first two words that come into your mind.

dancing _____   _____

mirror _____   _____

forgotten _____   _____

taxes _____   _____

Working It Out

Now we'll try some free writing sprints—short, fast races, using your pen instead of your feet. Several topics are listed below. Start writing on each topic, using the lines under it. Try to fill the lines in thirty seconds or less. Don't worry about spelling, grammar, or punctuation. Write until you fill all three lines and stop—even if you're in the middle of a word.

When I left home this morning I . . .

_____

_____

_____ **STOP!**

One thing I dislike about television is . . .

_____

_____

_____ **STOP!**

When I was a child, my best friend was . . .

_____

_____

_____ **STOP!**

The more you "warm up" for writing by free writing, the easier
every kind of writing will be.

✏️ *Writing On Your Own*

Next we'll try a longer race. Write continuously on the lines
below, setting down any words or ideas that come into your
head.

Today is _____ , the time is _____

and I am _____

_____

_____

_____ **STOP!**

You can do free writing on your own, in your journal. Try timing
yourself — write continuously for one minute, then four minutes,
and then ten minutes.

Here are some ideas to get started with. You can write about:
- the strangest person you ever met
- your first boyfriend/girlfriend
- your earliest memory from childhood
- what you would do with a million dollars
- an event in your life that changed you

▲ Looking Back

Do you get nervous when you know you have to write about
something? If you free write in your journal for fifteen minutes
every day, you will soon notice that writing isn't frightening any
more. Free writing helps you with any kind of writing you want
to do.

Learning New Words

> **In this lesson you will**
> ■ use context clues to add new words to your writing

Picture It

The cartoon above uses some made-up words: *biltrons,* *creeblop,* and *gondrords.* Which of the following words could replace the made-up words?

1. biltrons: a) anger   b) cold   c) tools

2. creeblop: a) floor   b) summer   c) peace

3. gondrords: a) popcorn   b) happy   c) movie stars

You've never seen these words before. But you can get an idea of their meaning from **context clues** in the cartoon. You find context clues by looking at the words before and after the word you don't know.

Here's an Example

You've seen how context clues can help you understand made-up words. Now context clues will help you understand some words from the GED Spelling List.

Joan visits her father *frequently.* She sees him once a week.

Frequently probably means   a) never   b) often   c) closer. Since Joan sees her father every week, we know it's wrong to say she *never* sees him. So *a* is incorrect. To say she visits him *closer* doesn't make sense, so *c* is incorrect. But she does see him *often,* as we can tell from the second sentence. So *b* is correct.

Now try a few more.

1. The baby eats all the time. He has a good *appetite.*
   Appetite probably means   a) love   b) happiness
   c) hunger.

2. Our garden is *flourishing.* We have lots of cucumbers, carrots, and tomatoes.
   Flourishing probably means   a) dying   b) changing
   c) growing well.

3. The band *omitted* the third verse of the song. They played only the first two verses.
   Omitted probably means   a) left out   b) wrote   c) sang.

4. The movie was a *tragedy.* In the end, the hero died.
   Tragedy probably means   a) a sad story   b) a funny story
   c) a boring story.

Working It Out

Read the following story. Use context clues to fill in the blanks with words from the word box.

Karen opened the door of her apartment. She was

_____ . "What happened?" she gasped,
       1

_____ into her living room. _____ and
       2   3

lamps were tipped over. Her sofa pillows were _____ .
                                                        4

Her books were thrown all over the _____ . Karen
                                              5

stared _____ the table where her television set
              6

usually stood. The _____ was gone. "I've been
                           7

_____ !" she screamed.
       8

Word Box	
at	chairs
floor	shocked
robbed	walking
ripped	television

Sometimes words have almost the same meaning, but are used differently. For example, *game* and *play* have similar meanings, but you wouldn't say "That was a great *play* of pool!" or "My children *game* together very well." In these next examples, use context clues to decide which word fits best in each sentence.

1a. Doctors are afraid Peggy's brain was _____ in the accident.   (broken, damaged)

1b. When Cindy left him, Ralph's heart was _____ .

2a. Tom's carelessness almost _____ him his life.   (cost, price)

2b. The sale _____ of this dress is twenty dollars.

3a. My children always _____ about sharing toys.   (debate, argue)

3b. The _____ between the candidates for mayor is at 8 P.M.

4a. Raul _____ his children a story before they go to bed.   (tells, says)

4b. Lillian _____ she'll be home tonight.

Writing On Your Own

On page 22 of this lesson, you used context clues to learn the meaning of *frequently, appetite, flourishing, omitted,* and *tragedy.* Now write five sentences on the lines below. Each sentence should use one of these new words.

1. _____
2. _____
3. _____
4. _____
5. _____

▲ Looking Back

When you read, context clues can help you learn new words. The more words you know, the better you will write.

Finding New Words

> *In this lesson you will*
> - learn ways to find new words
> - create word banks for new words
> - use the dictionary and other books to learn word meaning

Picture It

Would you let this mechanic repair *your* car? Probably not. He charges a lot of money. And he doesn't even know the *names* of what he's fixing!

Do you know the names of the parts of a car? What if you wanted to write about cars? Would you know where to find the **vocabulary** you needed? When you write on any topic, it helps to have the right words. In this lesson you'll learn a number of ways you can find and learn the words you need to know.

One way to learn new words is by starting a **word bank.** A word bank is a dictionary of words you want to use in speaking and writing.

Your journal is a good place for a word bank. In the back of your journal, set aside half a page for each letter of the alphabet. When you learn a new word, add it to your word bank in alphabetical order. Leave space around the word so you can add other words later. Next to your new word, write a short definition and a sentence using the word.

Here's an Example

Carol buys the newspaper once or twice a week. Each time she reads the paper, she looks for a few new words to add to her word bank. Here are the words she found one day.

foul   accused   stir-fried

This is what Carol wrote in her word bank:

A
accused   *blamed for something*
        Bill Smith was accused of robbing a bank.

F
foul   *in sports, something against the rules*
        The umpire called a foul on the pitcher.

S
stir-fried   fried in a little oil over high heat
        Chinese food is often stir-fried.

Working It Out

Before you start your own word bank, let's talk about how to look up new words.

Most of your new words will be in the **dictionary.** The dictionary lists words in alphabetical order. At the top of each page, there are two **guide words.** The guide words tell you the first and last words that are defined on the page.

Use this dictionary page to answer the questions below.

---

freedom | frog

freedom **1** the condition of being free. **2** liberty. *noun*

freeway a highway for fast driving on which no tolls are charged. *noun*

freeze **1** to harden by cold; turn into a solid. **2** to make or become very cold. *verb*

French **1** of or having to do with France, its people, or their language. **2** the people of France. **3** the language of France. 1 *adjective,* 2, 3 *noun*

friction a rubbing of one thing against another. *noun*

---

1. What are the **guide words** on this page?

_____   _____

2. Circle the words below that could also be on this page.

Friday   from   frequent   friend

3. Circle the word below that is spelled incorrectly.

freedem   freeze   friction

4. Which word could you use if you were writing about roads?

_____

5. Which word could you use if you were writing about France?

_____

Usually you can find out about a new word in a dictionary. But sometimes other books will be helpful.

For example, Carol couldn't find *stir-fried* in her dictionary. Instead, she found the meaning of *stir-fried* in a cookbook!

You may have books at home that will tell you about certain words. Some of these books are listed below. If you wanted to know more about the words given below, which book would you use? Write the letter of the book next to each list of words.

6. screwdriver, drill, wrench _____   **a)** cookbook

7. fever, aspirin, fainting _____   **b)** car owner's manual

8. turnip, seasoning, broil _____   **c)** home repair guide

9. clutch, spark plug, brake _____   **d)** first aid book

 *Writing On Your Own*

Now you can start your own word bank. For this exercise, you will need a newspaper or magazine and a dictionary. Look through the newspaper or magazine. Find six new words. Write each word in the blanks below. Next to the word, write a short definition and a sentence using the word. An example is given.

Word	Definition and Sentence
passport	*a document showing what country you're from*
	Lisa needed her passport so she could go to Spain.

Now prepare the pages for your word bank in your journal. Copy the new words, their definitions, and your sentences on the correct pages of your word bank. Try to add new words every week.

▲ Looking Back

A good **vocabulary** improves your reading, speaking, and writing skills. You can find new vocabulary words in the newspaper, in your favorite magazines, or even on billboards! When you find a new word, add it to your word bank. Use the word when you speak or write. You're on your way to expanding your vocabulary!

Grouping New Words

In this lesson you will
■ use word lists and word maps to group words for writing

Getting Started

In Lessons 5 and 6 you practiced skills for learning new words. Now you'll learn how to group words together as you get ready to write. You'll learn how to make word lists and word maps.

In a **word list,** you list all the words you can think of that go with a certain topic.

On a **word map,** you show *how* the words on a word list go together.

Here's an Example

Sam wanted to write about painting a room. First, he made a **word list.** He wrote down all the words he could think of that went with "painting a room."

Painting a Room

window frames	doors	paint thinner	scraping
paint	ceiling	rags	sponge
roller	walls	caulk	water
patching	floor	cleaning	soap
paint scraper	sandpaper	brushes	painting

Next, Sam wanted to see how the words on his word list went together, so he made a **word map.**

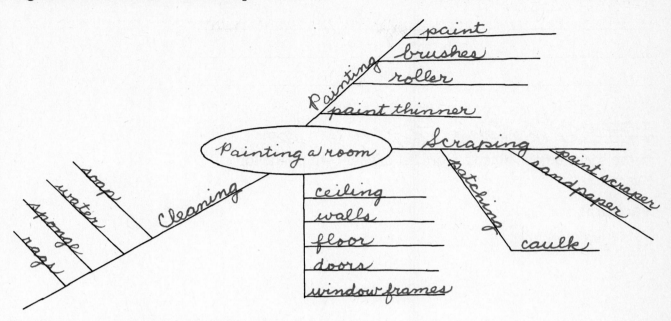

Sam's word map put his words in order. When he starts writing, his job will be easier.

You can start word lists on topics you want to write about. Remember, each list is on a different topic. You might have a list for car words, one for cooking words, and one for nature words. Keep a folder for your word lists.

When you are ready to write about a certain topic, then it's time to make a word map.

Working It Out

Here are two word lists on the topics "Housecleaning" and "Taking the Bus." Fill in the empty blanks by adding more words to each list.

Housecleaning

dusting   broom   mop

_____   _____   _____

_____   _____   _____

_____   _____   _____

Taking the Bus

passengers   bus stop   standing

_____   _____   _____

_____   _____   _____

_____   _____   _____

✏️ *Writing On Your Own*

In the space below, make a word list of your own on the topic
"Vacation."

Vacation

Next, choose one of the three word lists you have written in this
lesson. Make a word map on the same topic. Use the words from
your list. You can also add new words.

▲ Looking Back

When you write, it's important to use the right words. Word lists
and word maps will help you do just that.

Getting the Details Right

In this lesson you will
- learn to use details in your writing

Picture It

Look at the pictures on the right. Milo is a portrait artist. When he draws a face, he first draws an outline. Then he fills in details so that his drawing comes alive.

An artist works step by step. With each step, the artist adds a few more details. Good writing is also done in steps. With each step, you add details. The details make your writing come alive.

In the last few lessons, you've learned a lot about finding and using new words. You can use these words to add details to your writing. **Details** are small bits of information about a topic.

Here's an Example

Clara walked past the house.

Clara walked past the large brick house.

Clara walked slowly past the large brick house, admiring its beauty.

The first sentence doesn't give you much information. The second sentence tells you the house is large and brick. The third sentence tells you about the house *and* about Clara. It says Clara walked *slowly* and she was *admiring* the house. The **details** help us get a better picture.

Working It Out

Rewrite the following sentences. Add descriptive details. The first one is done for you.

1. The policewoman spoke to the girl.

~~The policewoman~~ spoke gently to the frightened girl.

2. The bear chased the dogs.

_____

3. The spy left the airport.

_____

4. The sun rose over the mountains.

_____

Artists often draw the objects closest to them—books on a desk, food on a countertop, or clothes in a closet.

You can practice adding details to your writing in the same way. Try describing the chair you're sitting in right now. What color is it? What shape? What does it feel like? What kind of noise does it make when you move it? Below, list at least four words or phrases that describe your chair.

_____ _____ _____ _____

We experience the world around us through our **five senses**—through **seeing, hearing, smelling, tasting,** and **touching.** When we give details about something we can use **sense words**—words that describe the object through our five senses.

Look at the words you wrote down to describe your chair. Circle any that are **sense words.** Can you think of any more sense words that describe your chair? Write them in the margins.

Think of one of your closets at home. What are some sense words that would describe the inside of the closet? Write the words in the blanks below.

_____ _____ _____ _____

_____ _____ _____ _____

 *Writing On Your Own*

Imagine you are at a large outdoor party. It is summer. What would you see? hear? smell? taste? touch? Write down at least three words or phrases for each sense. An example in each category is given.

Seeing	Hearing	Smelling	Tasting	Touching
green grass	*sizzling coals*	*juicy steaks*	*hot mustard*	*wet napkin*
_____	_____	_____	_____	_____
_____	_____	_____	_____	_____
_____	_____	_____	_____	_____

Now try writing a few sentences describing this imaginary party. Use the words from your list. Talk about the food, the people, the music—bring the party to life.

_____

_____

_____

_____

_____

Make lists of descriptive words for each of the senses. Add the lists to your word list folder. A **thesaurus** can help you find sense words for your lists. When you look up a word in a thesaurus it will tell you other words that mean almost the same thing. So, for example, you can look up *smooth* in a thesaurus. You might find the words *polished, sleek, slippery,* and *silky.* The next time you want to describe something that is smooth, you will have more words to choose from!

▲ Looking Back

Often we use only *seeing* words to describe something. But we have four other senses, too! The next time you describe something, remember to tell how it *sounded, tasted, smelled,* and *felt.*

The Naming Words: Nouns

In this lesson you will:

- learn what nouns are
- practice using rules to capitalize proper nouns

Getting Started

Read the following statement. Fill in the blanks with things that, in your opinion, the world would be better off without. An example is given.

- I think the world would be a better place without:

bugs _____ _____ _____

 _____ _____ _____

Did you fill every blank with things you'd like to get rid of? Each word you wrote is a noun.

> A **noun** is a word that names a person, place, thing, or idea.

Look at the words listed below and underline the nouns.

poverty	sunshine	Lake Tahoe	kitchen
arrange	quickly	pour	disappear
marriage	bury	Conrad Braun	career
Maple Street	great	jealous	happiness

> A **proper noun** is a noun that names a **particular** person, place, thing, or idea. Proper nouns are **capitalized.**

Turn back to the word list. Can you find the proper nouns? Underline them twice.

When you write, sometimes it's hard to tell if a word is a proper noun and should be capitalized. The next section will give you six rules for capitalization and examples of each rule.

Here's an Example

Read through the following rules. Decide if the sentences after each rule show correct capitalization. If the capitalization is correct, write *OK* in the margin. If the capitalization is wrong, fix it. The first one is done for you.

▶ **Rule 1:** Capitalize the **names** of persons, historical events and periods, and the official names of groups or organizations. EXAMPLES: Edwin Blanchard, Carol Kline, the Civil War, the Rotary Club, the Internal Revenue Service

   1. Many soldiers lost their lives in world war two.
                                 W   W T

   2. Franklin Roosevelt was president during the great depression.

   3. My friend Paula used to work for Amoco.

▶ **Rule 2:** Capitalize **titles** if they are part of a person's name.
EXAMPLE: Today Governor Blixen will speak.
Do not capitalize titles if they are used as common nouns.
EXAMPLE: Today the governor will speak.

   4. Grace Kelly became a Princess when she married Prince Rainier.

   5. Nathan Bradley would like to become Mayor.

   6. We invited Dr. Ortiz, Mayor Todd, and the president.

▶ **Rule 3:** Capitalize the **names** of countries, nationalities, religions, and languages. EXAMPLES: France, Vietnamese, Lutheran, Arabic

   7. My family celebrates all the jewish holidays.

   8. She learned to speak german in school.

   9. The philippines once belonged to Spain.

  10. The chinese who settled in America were hard workers.

▶ **Rule 4:** Capitalize the **names** of geographic regions and bodies of water. EXAMPLES: the South Side of Milwaukee, the Pacific Northwest, Lake Erie

Do not capitalize north, south, east, or west when they are only showing direction. EXAMPLE: Go south for one mile.

11. The Mississippi River is east of here.

12. Many oil tankers cross the atlantic ocean.

13. Newark is in the East.

14. The Midwest has miles and miles of good farmland.

▶ **Rule 5:** Capitalize the **names** of streets, buildings, bridges, parks, cities, counties, and states. EXAMPLES: Hansberry Drive, the Sears Tower, the Brooklyn Bridge, Cooper Park, Minneapolis, Brown County, Ohio

15. The Millers live near central park in New York.

16. The Building on the corner is two hundred years old.

17. The Westons live on Munster avenue.

▶ **Rule 6:** Capitalize the **names** of months and days. EXAMPLES: July, December, Sunday, Friday

Do not capitalize the seasons of the year. EXAMPLE: Aiko will visit Japan in the fall.

18. During the Winter, I usually gain weight.

19. Even though it's October, it still seems like summer.

Working It Out

Read the following paragraph and decide which words need to be capitalized. Rewrite the paragraph correctly on a separate sheet of paper.

■ Last summer greg went to california to visit his grandmother. She lives in oakland, which is east of san francisco. One day greg and his grandmother drove across the golden gate bridge. After hearing about it for many years, greg was happy to finally see the world-famous bridge.

✏️ Writing On Your Own

The form below is an opinion survey. It asks you questions about the things you like. It also asks for some general information about you. Fill in the information. Decide whether each answer needs to be capitalized.

At the end of each sentence, fill in the number of the rule that helped you make your decision about capitalization.

My full name is _____ . (Rule ____)

The date of my birth is _____ , 19____ . (Rule ____)

The place I was born is called _____ . (Rule ____)

The three states I would most like to visit are _____ ,

_____ , and _____ .   (Rule ____)

My favorite city is _____ . (Rule ____)

My favorite season of the year is _____ . (Rule ____)

My favorite musician is _____ . (Rule ____)

If I were in politics, I would like to be elected

_____ . (Rule ____)

An Idea to Remember

Are the rules for capitalization confusing? Try out the "only one" rule. When you are deciding whether to capitalize a word or phrase, ask yourself: Is there only one of them? If there is, **capitalize** it. For example, there are many rivers, but only one Mississippi River. There are many presidents, but only one President Washington. If you can't remember all the rules, remember the "only one" rule.

▲ Looking Back

You use **nouns** every time you write. They are the words that name persons, places, and things. If you use a *particular* name, you're using a **proper noun.** Remember to start a proper noun with a capital letter.

The Replacing Words: Pronouns

> *In this lesson you will*
> ■ match pronouns to nouns and other pronouns
> ■ learn to use pronouns clearly

Getting Started

In Lesson 9 you learned about nouns and proper nouns. Now we will talk about **pronouns.**

Read the following paragraph. What words could replace the underlined words?

■ The Randalls are my neighbors. <u>The Randalls'</u> daughter Anne plays the electric guitar. <u>Anne</u> practices several hours a day. <u>Anne's</u> guitar is so loud that my window rattles. In fact, I'm afraid <u>my window</u> will break!

You could replace the underlined words with the pronouns *their, she, her,* and *it.* A **pronoun** stands in for a noun or sometimes for other pronouns.

Here is a list of pronouns that we use often in writing or conversation.

I	me	my, mine	**Special Singular Pronouns:**	
you		your, yours	one	somebody
he	him	his	someone	everybody
she	her	hers	everyone	nobody
it		its	each	anybody

In the next section, you'll learn how to use pronouns correctly.

Here's an Example

Pronouns have to **agree** with the nouns or pronouns they replace. In other words, if the word a pronoun replaces is **singular** (only one), the pronoun must also be **singular.** If the word a pronoun replaces is **plural** (more than one), the pronoun must also be **plural.** Look at this sentence.

- *Everybody* should look carefully before buying a car, so *they* can get a good price.

In this sentence, the pronoun *everybody* is singular. It is one of the special singular pronouns listed above. These pronouns *look* plural, but they are really singular. In this sentence, *everybody* does not agree with the plural pronoun *they.*
   Now look at the next sentence.

- Used *cars* are cheaper than new cars, but can anybody trust *it*?

In this sentence, the pronoun *it* is singular. But it is referring back to the noun *cars,* which is plural. *It* and *used cars* do not agree.
   Here is a corrected version of the two sentences.

- *Everybody* should look carefully before buying a car, so *he or she* can get a good price. Used *cars* are cheaper than new cars, but can anybody trust *them*?

Is the meaning of the next paragraph clear?

- Decide whether you want power steering and power brakes. *They* make it easier to stop quickly.

Does *they* refer to power steering *and* power brakes? Or to power brakes only? The pronoun *they* is unclear in meaning.

- **Correct:** Decide whether you want power steering and power brakes. *Power brakes* make it easier to stop quickly.

Is the next sentence clear?

- Paul's children have hamsters and *they* don't smell.

Who doesn't smell? The children or the hamsters? Again, the word *they* is unclear.

- **Correct:** Paul's children's hamsters don't smell.

Working It Out

Fill in the blanks below with the correct pronoun. The first one is done for you.

1. I own a car.

   It is _____*my*_____ car, and I take care of ___*it*___ .

2. Jay will ask Sue for a date.

   _____ will ask _____ out tomorrow.

3. We have a son.

   _____ son wants a bicycle for _____ birthday.

4. Lisa has new glasses.

   _____ bought _____ two weeks ago.

5. You gave a sock to the dog.

   _____ sock is in _____ mouth.

In the sentences below, the underlined pronouns are incorrect or unclear. Rewrite the sentences correctly on the lines below. The first one is done for you.

6. One should think before <u>you</u> act.

   One should think before one acts. _____

7. Someone left <u>their</u> dress on the floor.

   _____

8. Jack called Ed yesterday. <u>He</u> has a cold.

   _____

9. My neighbors have cats. I don't let <u>them</u> in my house.

   _____

10. That car has <u>their</u> headlights on.

    _____

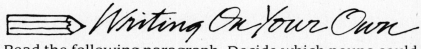 *Writing On Your Own*

Read the following paragraph. Decide which nouns could be replaced by pronouns, and which pronouns are used incorrectly. Rewrite the paragraph with your corrections on the lines below.

■ Credit cards are popular in the United States. Many people use credit cards often. Be careful, however, when you buy something with a credit card. Unless you pay for them quickly, you are charged a high rate of interest. A credit card can be helpful, but a credit card can also be expensive.

_____

_____

_____

_____

_____

_____

Here's a way to practice using nouns and pronouns. In your journal, write a few sentences describing some of the people in your family. Tell who they are, what they are like, and what they do. Remember to capitalize all the proper nouns.

When you finish, go back and underline all the nouns. Ask yourself, ''Can I replace any of these nouns with pronouns?''

Then circle all the pronouns. Ask yourself, ''Are my pronouns clear in meaning? Does each one agree with the word it replaces?'' Make corrections and rewrite the sentences in your journal.

▲ Looking Back

Why do people use pronouns? Pronouns are shortcuts. Instead of saying, ''Leo and Rose said Leo and Rose would paint Leo and Rose's kitchen today,'' you can simply say, ''Leo and Rose said they would paint their kitchen today.'' Isn't that easier?

The Matching Game: Subjects and Verbs

> *In this lesson you will*
> - learn about subjects and verbs
> - learn and use the rules for subject/verb agreement

Picture It

Use the picture to complete the following sentences.

_____rides two horses.

A bear on roller skates _____ .

What did you add to each sentence? In the first sentence, you had to say *who* or *what* was riding two horses. In other words, you had to add the **subject.**

> The **subject** of a sentence is the person or thing doing the action.

In the second sentence, you had to say what the bear was *doing*. In other words, you had to add the **verb.**

> The **verb** tells the action in a sentence.

Every sentence needs a subject and a verb. The subject and the verb have to agree with each other—in other words, they have to match. Can you match these subjects with the right verbs?

Subjects	Verbs
_____ 1. the children	**a.** play
_____ 2. the high school teachers	**b.** plays
_____ 3. the baby	**c.** teach
_____ 4. the college professor	**d.** teaches

Could you match the subjects and verbs correctly? You probably noticed that each verb was written two different ways.

Sometimes verbs must change to agree with the subject.

Here's an Example

Read this column   **Complete this column**

Read this column	Complete this column
I run	I think
you run	you _____
he ⎫	he ⎫
she ⎬ runs	she ⎬ _____
it ⎭	it ⎭
we run	we _____
they run	they _____

Did you notice that when the subject is *he, she,* or *it,* the verb adds *-s*? When the subject is *I, you, we,* or *they,* the verb does not change.

When a verb ends in *o, s, x, z, ch,* or *sh,* the rule is slightly different. You add *-es* to these verbs when the subject is *he, she,* or *it.*

Read this column	Complete this column
I do	I reach
you do	you _____
he ⎫	he ⎫
she ⎬ do**es**	she ⎬ _____
it ⎭	it ⎭
we do	we _____
they do	they _____

Now, what if the subject is like one of these?

Mary and Kate   the morning   six firefighters   Karl

Subject/Verb Agreement

If the subject of a sentence can be replaced by *he, she,* or *it,* the verb adds an *-s* or *-es* ending.

Examples: *It*
           ~~The dog~~ barks all night long.

           He
           ~~Jason~~ talks on the telephone a lot.

If the subject can be replaced by *they,* the verb doesn't change.

Examples: *They*
           ~~The watchdogs~~ bark at strangers.

           They
           ~~Pam and Charlie~~ talk to each other every day.

Working It Out

Rewrite the following sentences and insert the correct verbs.

1. You (does/do) not know me, and he (does/do) know me.

---

2. He (likes/like) Debbie a lot, and we (likes/like) her too.

---

3. I (agrees/agree) with Marvin and he (agrees/agree) with me.

Cross out the subject of each sentence below. Decide whether it can be replaced by *he, she, it,* or *they.* Write the replacement above the subject. Then underline the correct verb form. The first one is done for you.

   It
1. ~~Our old refrigerator~~ (needs/need) a new motor.

2. Bridget (wants/want) to vacation in Mexico this winter.

3. The neighbors (goes/go) out of town every weekend.

✏️➔ *Writing On Your Own*

Here are two **irregular** verbs—verbs that don't follow the rules. Notice that the verb form for *he, she,* and *it* still ends in *-s.*

be		**have**	
I **am**	we **are**	I **have**	we **have**
you **are**	they **are**	you **have**	they **have**
he		he	
she ⟩ **is**		she ⟩ **has**	
it		it	

Write out the following sentences using the correct form of the verbs *have* or *be.* The first one is done for you.

1. I _____(be)_____ tired of working.

I am tired of working.

2. Donald _____(have)_____ a terrible cold.

_____

3. The horses _____(be)_____ in the meadow.

_____

4. We _____(have)_____ three small children.

_____

Copy the following paragraph on a separate sheet of paper, choosing the correct verb form for each sentence.

- At three A.M., Bruno Ponti (parks/park) his ambulance outside Diana's home. "We (has/have) to hurry!" say her frightened parents. The ambulance (speeds/speed) toward the hospital. Minutes later, doctors and nurses (is/are) working to save Diana's life.

▲ Looking Back

Matching subjects to verbs is something you do in conversation all the time, without even thinking about it. Now you know the rules for doing it correctly.

Yesterday, Today, and Tomorrow: Verb Times

> *In this lesson you will*
> - learn how verbs show time in the past, present, and future
> - write sentences using different verb times

Picture It

Look at the cartoon. What happened *yesterday*? (I *fought*.) What happens *today*? (I *fight*.) What will happen *tomorrow*? (I *will fight*.) Verbs tell us the **time** of sentences. *Fought, fight,* and *will fight* are the **past, present,** and **future times** of the verb *fight*.

In the last lesson you learned how to make verbs agree with their subjects. In this lesson you'll learn how to use verbs to show past, present, or future time.

Here's an Example

Five verb times are listed below, each with two examples.
Complete the second example using the verb *clean*.

[1] present event

Nadia plays the piano now.

or

Nadia is playing the piano now.

Sergio _____his apartment now.
or

Sergio _____ _____ his apartment now.

[2] future event

Nadia will play the piano next week.

Sergio _____ _____ his apartment next
week.

[3] past event

Nadia played the piano yesterday.

Sergio _____ his apartment yesterday.

[4] past and continuing event

Nadia has played the piano for many years.

Sergio _____ _____ his apartment many
times.

[5] past event before another past event

Nadia had played the piano before she played the violin.

Sergio _____ _____ his apartment
before he went out.

Play and *clean* are **regular verbs**—verbs that follow the rules.
Here are the rules for regular verbs:

---

1. Add *-s* or *-es* to regular verbs to make the **present time**
when the subject is *he, she,* or *it*. EXAMPLE: Sally sing*s*.
2. Add *-ed* to regular verbs to make the three **past times**.
EXAMPLES: Blake sneez*ed*. Blake *has* sneez*ed*. Blake *had*
sneez*ed*.
3. Add the **helping verb** *will* to make the **future time**.
EXAMPLE: Tamara *will* call.

In the following sentences, use context clues to decide on the correct verb time. Underline your answer. The first one is done for you.

1. Years ago Margaret (dance/<u>danced</u>) whenever she could.
2. Next month the class (studied/will study) nutrition.
3. Before she moved away from home, Leticia (starts/had started) saving money.
4. For many years the Schmidts (have loved/will love) to travel.
5. Every time Donald speaks he (bores/had bored) everyone.

Working It Out

The next chart shows eight **irregular verbs**—verbs that do *not* follow the rules.

Irregular Verbs

Present		Past		Future
Use with *I, you, we, they*, and plural nouns	Use with *he, she, it*, and singular nouns	Use alone	Use with helping verbs *has, have, had*	Use with helping verb *will*
am, are	is	was, were	been	be
begin	begins	began	begun	begin
do	does	did	done	do
eat	eats	ate	eaten	eat
go	goes	went	gone	go
have	has	had	had	have
see	sees	saw	seen	see
take	takes	took	taken	take

Use the chart to check each of the following sentences. If the underlined verb is correct, write *correct* in the blank next to the sentence. If the underlined verb is incorrect, write the correct verb in the blank.

_____ 1. William <u>seen</u> a good movie last night.

_____ 2. Linda and Denise <u>have ate</u> all the pizza.

_____ 3. Albert <u>goes</u> to Florida every winter.

_____ 4. We <u>done</u> all the kitchen remodeling ourselves.

_____ **5.** It <u>take</u> time to build a friendship.

_____ **6.** Before she went to Germany, Andrea <u>had began</u> to study German.

_____ **7.** Francesca <u>have</u> a baby in two more months.

_____ **8.** The keys <u>were</u> still in the car.

Change the following sentences from the past to the future.

1. The band tried to keep the crowd happy.

_____

2. The ranger has seen many unusual birds in the forest.

_____

3. Peter had studied all week for the exam.

_____

Writing On Your Own

In the news article below, each sentence has one error in verb time. Rewrite the article and correct each error on a separate sheet of paper.

■ One week ago the Farmers' Trust Bank will announce it is buying the Jasper farm on Rte. 17. "We been working on this farm for seventy years," said Joe Jasper. "Now we have saw our land sold to someone else."

It be unclear if the Jaspers will move. Last week bank president Albert Givson say, "We need someone to grow crops on that land. Maybe the Jaspers will wanted to stay."

▲ Looking Back

After you write a paragraph, go back and see whether your verbs are correct. Make sure your verbs show past, present or future time correctly.

Using Active and Concrete Verbs

In this lesson you will
- practice writing with active, concrete verbs

Picture It

Which of these paragraphs is more exciting?

- In Paris we were followed by two men in black raincoats. We went down a side street, but they were still there. We were getting nervous because of them. We hoped they wouldn't do anything to us.
- In Paris two men in black raincoats followed us. We ducked down a side street, but they hurried after us. They made us nervous. We hoped they wouldn't attack us.

Did you choose the second paragraph? The *verbs* make it more interesting. You can use verbs the same way.

Here's an Example

Compare these two sentences.

paragraph 1	**paragraph 2**
"In Paris we *were followed* by two men in black raincoats."	"In Paris two men in black raincoats *followed* us."

In paragraph 2 the verb is **active.** The subject of the sentence is *doing* the action, not *receiving* it. This makes the sentence more interesting.

Now compare these sentences.

paragraph 1	paragraph 2
"We *went* down a side street, but they *were* still there."	"We *ducked* down a side street, but they *hurried* after us."

The verbs *went* and *were* in paragraph 1 don't give a very clear picture of what happened. The verbs *ducked* and *hurried* in paragraph 2 give a sharper idea of the action—a more **concrete** picture of what happened.

Two Hints for Exciting Writing
1. Make your verbs *active.*
2. Make your verbs *concrete.*

Notice that the second paragraph is shorter. You don't always need a lot of words to describe something—in fact, it's often better to use *fewer* words. When you use active, concrete verbs, your sentences will be more *concise*—shorter and to the point.

Working It Out

Rewrite the following sentences so that the verb is **active.** Notice the verb time in the sentence and write your sentence in the same time. The first one is done for you.

1. The window <u>was broken</u> by Leah. (past)

Leah broke the window.

2. The dessert <u>will be prepared</u> by Chef Raoul. (future)

_____

3. The banners <u>were carried</u> by the marchers. (past)

_____

4. We <u>are</u> always <u>being watched</u> by our neighbors. (present)

_____

5. "Another Love" <u>is sung</u> by Toni Johnson. (present)

_____

Rewrite the following sentences so that the verb is more **concrete**. Use the same verb time. The first one is done for you.

1. Mrs. Nilsson <u>comes</u> down the road. (present)

Mrs. Nilsson skips down the road.

2. "I can't find my wallet," Art <u>says</u>. (present)

_____

3. The birds <u>took</u> all the seeds I planted. (past)

_____

4. Corey <u>went</u> into the tunnel. (past)

_____

5. Andre <u>will get</u> some money. (future)

_____

✏️➡ *Writing On Your Own*

The following paragraph finishes the story about the two men in black raincoats. Rewrite the paragraph on a separate sheet of paper, changing each underlined verb into an active, concrete verb. Change each sentence to fit the new verb.

■ We <u>got</u> to a cafe and ordered coffee. The men in black raincoats <u>came</u> too. We <u>were</u> still <u>being watched</u> by them. We <u>were frightened</u> by their presence. Suddenly we <u>were spoken</u> to by one of them, who asked, "Aren't you the Prince and Princess of Liechtenstein?" "Certainly not!" I <u>said</u>. "Well, what a waste of time!" he <u>said</u>, and the two men quickly left the cafe.

▲ Looking Back

Concrete, active verbs will make your writing more interesting. Use words that give clear pictures of what you mean.

Writing in Sentences

Beginnings and Endings

In this lesson you will
- learn to capitalize the letter that begins a sentence
- learn to end every sentence with a period, question mark, or exclamation point

Getting Started

So far you have worked a lot in this book with writing the right **words.** Now you're ready to write **sentences.** Start by looking at how you *begin* and *end* every sentence you write. First, read what happened to Laura.

- "Oh, Mother, Grandma wants us to stop the wedding!" Laura sobbed. "Let me see that telegram!" her mother said. It read:

    I AM THINKING OF YOU TODAY STOP THE WEDDING
    IS A SPECIAL DAY FOR ALL STOP LOVE GRANDMA
    "It's all right, Laura. Grandma isn't trying to stop the wedding!" her mother laughed. "It's just that telegrams use the word STOP between sentences!"

What was Grandma really saying?
Laura would have understood her grandmother's message if the telegram had used periods instead of the word STOP. When you write, you show where sentences begin and end by doing two things. You **capitalize** the letter that begins the sentence. You mark the end of the sentence with a **period,** a **question mark,** or an **exclamation point.**

Here's an Example

Stewart wrote the following paragraph about his baby son:

- Michael is my first child, and I am proud of him he is six months old even though he's so little, he loves the water when he is a few months older, we will take him to swimming classes at the YMCA.

Stewart rewrote his paragraph and divided it into sentences. This is how it looked after he made the corrections:

- Michael is my first child, and I am proud of him. He is six months old. Even though he's so little, he loves the water. When he is a few months older, we will take him to swimming classes at the YMCA.

An Idea to Remember

- Every sentence begins with a **capital letter.**
- Every sentence ends with a **period,** a **question mark,** or an **exclamation point.**

In this lesson we'll talk only about sentences that end with periods. In the next lesson you'll learn when to use question marks and exclamation points.

Working It Out

Read the following two paragraphs. Show where each sentence begins and ends by capitalizing the first letter and placing a period at the end of the sentence. The first sentence is done for you.

- W
  when you have a job interview, remember these
  suggestions first of all, dress neatly don't wear blue jeans
  or tennis shoes second, don't chew gum or smoke third,
  find out about the company ahead of time write down some
  questions to ask during the interview to show your interest
  in the business finally, after the interview, write a short
  note or call the company to thank the people for spending
  time with you mention again how much you'd like to work
  for the company

- every four years, the people of the United States elect a president the two major political parties, the Democrats and the Republicans, each pick a candidate these candidates are chosen at a national convention a few months before the election although there are always candidates from other, smaller political parties, it would be quite surprising if someone other than a Democrat or a Republican became president

✏️➤ *Writing On Your Own*

Add words to make each of the following phrases into a sentence. Be sure to capitalize the first letter and put a period at the end of each sentence. The first one is done for you.

1. before we thought about it

Before we thought about it, we said yes.

2. singing at the Christmas concert

3. the cat, damp and shivering

4. since Carla was frightened

5. said the party was Friday

Now write a few sentences of your own. Use your own paper. Write on this topic: Do you think women should be allowed to run for president? Why or why not? Be sure to capitalize the beginning of each sentence and put a period at the end.

▲ Looking Back

If you have trouble telling where sentences begin and end, read your writing out loud. Your voice will want to pause at the place where a new sentence begins.

Exploring Types of Sentences

In this lesson you will

■ practice writing statements, questions, commands, and exclamations

Picture It

I think I'll say, "Mr. Paulsen, would you consider giving me a raise?"

I'm going to say, "Mr. Paulsen, I need a raise."

I'll say, "Look here, Paulsen, give me a raise."

Mr. Paulsen, ... uh ... I just love this job!

When you have something to say, there are different ways of saying it. You can ask a question, make a statement, give a command, or make an exclamation. In this lesson you'll learn how to write statements, questions, commands, and exclamations.

■ A **statement** gives information. Example: I want a raise.

■ A **question** asks about something. Example: Do I need a raise?

■ A **command** gives an order. Example: Give me a raise.

■ An **exclamation** shows strong feeling. Example: I got a raise!

Remember to use the correct end punctuation for each sentence type. Statements end with a period (.). Questions end with a question mark (?). Commands end with a period or an exclamation point (!). Exclamations end with an exclamation point.

Here's an Example

Roberto wrote four sentences on the topic of opening day at the baseball stadium.

Statement: I always go to opening day at the baseball stadium.

Question: Are you going to opening day at the stadium?

Command: Go to the opening day baseball game.

Exclamation: It's opening day!

You can change sentences from one form into another. For example, you can change a statement into a question.

Statement: The trains are late because of the accident.

Question: Are the trains late because of the accident?

or: Why are the trains late?

You can also change a question into a statement.

Question: When will Carrie's band play?

Statement: Carrie's band will play on Thursday night.

Working It Out

Read each of the following sentences. If it is a statement, change it into a question. If it is a question, turn it into a statement. The first one is done for you.

1. On Sundays the prisoners can have visitors.

When can the prisoners have visitors?

2. Is there a doctor on the plane?

_____

3. We can't go swimming because it's too cold.

_____

4. Do the Tanakas have any children?

_____

5. The eggs are in the refrigerator.

_____

In command sentences, the **subject** does not actually appear in the sentence. The subject of every command sentence is *you*. For example, "Get the phone" really means "*You* get the phone."

Change the following statements and questions into commands. The first one is done for you.

1. I wish you would stop teasing your sister.

  Stop teasing your sister.

2. Could you turn left at the next light?

_____

3. You should save more money.

_____

4. Will you bring me the newspaper?

_____

✎➤ *Writing On Your Own*

Look at the picture. Write a statement, a question, a command, and an exclamation about what you see in the picture.

1. Statement: _____

_____

2. Question: _____

_____

3. Command: _____

_____

4. Exclamation: _____

_____

▲ Looking Back

Listen to yourself talk to your friends. Are you a person who asks a lot of questions? Do you like to give commands? Do you make a lot of exclamations? The kind of sentences you use might tell you something about your personality!

Completing Your Sentences

> *In this lesson you will*
> - learn the elements of a complete sentence
> - write complete sentences

Getting Started

You know that every sentence has a **subject** (the person or thing doing the action) and a **verb** (the action). Every sentence also has a **complete, independent** thought—an idea that stands alone.

What happens when the subject, verb, or complete, independent thought is missing? Read about Fred.

- Fred, a newspaper reporter, went to Wally's Wagon, a popular new restaurant. He asked four people, ''Why do you like to eat at Wally's Wagon?'' They said:
  ''Because of the people.''
  ''Since it's pretty cheap.''
  ''A good location.''
  ''Because it's open till midnight.''
This is the story Fred wrote:

Wally's Wagon
Because of the people. Since it's pretty cheap. A good location. Because it's open till midnight.

When Fred's boss read the story, she said, ''Maybe *you* can understand this. No one else will unless you write it in **complete sentences.**''

Here's an Example

Read the next line. Is it a complete sentence?

■ Because the old man looked tired.

This example has a subject (*the old man*) and a verb (*looked*).
But it does *not* have a complete, independent thought. Suppose
someone walked up to you and said, "Because the old man
looked tired." You might say, "Well, what? What happened?"
The idea in this example cannot stand alone. This is a **sentence
fragment.**

You can change sentence fragments into sentences by *adding*
words or *taking away* words. See how the last example can be
corrected.

Complete Sentence: Because the old man looked tired, *Lisa
gave him her seat on the bus.*

Complete Sentence: The old man looked tired.

Now it's your turn. Use the following sentence fragment to write
two complete sentences. Write the first sentence by adding
words. Write the second sentence by taking away words.

■ After Leslie saw the doctor.

1. _____

2. _____

Working It Out

Decide whether each of the following is a sentence or a
sentence fragment. If it is a sentence, write "S" in the blank. If
it is a fragment, write "F."

_____ 1. Parking is a problem in our city.

_____ 2. With so few parking spaces, many parking tickets
given.

_____ 3. Almost every driver has received one or two of them.

_____ 4. One man, however, beat all the records.

_____ 5. Two hundred and fifty-two tickets in Clarence
Parker's name.

_____ 6. Clarence was shocked.

_____ 7. Asked his three teenage children about it.

_____ 8. Since they also used the car.

_____ 9. His children had gotten all the tickets.

_____ 10. Why he made them pay the fines.

Make each of the following sentence fragments into a complete sentence. The first one is done for you.

1. Because Pete wants the lowest prices.

   Because Pete wants the lowest prices, he shops at Savemore.

2. The old house, full of bats and spiders.

   _____

3. Whenever Jim and Felicia call us back.

   _____

4. Talked in her sleep.

   _____

5. Without noticing the traffic light.

   _____

6. From the moment we walked in the door.

   _____

7. Since Susan and Greg are going.

   _____

8. Felt happy.

   _____

 *Writing On Your Own*

The following paragraph has two sentence fragments. Rewrite the paragraph, changing the sentence fragments into complete sentences. Use your own paper.

- Do you know how to relax? Walking a good way. To get away from your problems. Walking can give you time to think things through.

In your journal, write a few complete sentences about a problem in your neighborhood. Tell what the problem is. Then give some ideas on how to deal with it.

▲ Looking Back

When you talk, complete sentences aren't necessary. But when you write, only **complete sentences** will get your ideas across.

Reining In Your Sentences

> **In this lesson you will**
> ■ learn to identify and correct run-on sentences and comma splices

Picture It

> "...so then I say, "OK, Willie, why don't you come over on Saturday and we'll clean out the garage" and he says "Well, I don't know, I told Alice we might take a drive" and I say, "Come on, Willie! It'll probably rain on Saturday and besides, we can watch the game" and he says..."

Have you ever met someone who didn't know when to stop talking? It can be very tiring to listen to people like that. Some people, though, don't know when to stop *writing*. Their sentences run on and on. That's why we call their sentences **run-on sentences.**

Another mistake some writers make is called a comma splice. A **comma splice** happens when two complete, independent thoughts are connected with a comma.

Here's an Example

Run-on sentence	Malcolm would not get lost in the woods he has hunted there for twenty years.
Corrected	Malcolm would not get lost in the woods; he has hunted there for twenty years. or Malcolm would not get lost in the woods. He has hunted there for twenty years.

There are many ways you can fix run-on sentences. Two are shown above. The two complete thoughts can be divided by a **semicolon (;)** or by a **period.**

You could also fix this sentence by adding a **connecting word.** You could say, "Malcolm would not get lost in the woods since he has hunted there for twenty years."

Comma splice	Denise loves to fish, she is out on the river almost every weekend.
Corrected	Denise loves to fish; she is out on the river almost every weekend. or Denise loves to fish. She is out on the river almost every weekend.

The comma in the original sentence separates two complete thoughts. But a comma isn't enough. You can correct the comma splice by using a **semicolon** or a **period.** Sometimes you can correct a comma splice by adding a **connecting word.**

Working It Out

Remember, you *can* use a comma to separate parts of a sentence when one part is dependent on the other. Ask yourself: "Can this part of the sentence stand alone?" If it can't, it is **dependent** on the main clause.

Correct: Because we had forgotten the money, we went home.
   Why: "Because we had forgotten the money" is a dependent thought. A comma is therefore correct.

Read the following sentences. Write "correct," "run-on," or "comma splice" in each blank. The first one is done for you.

run-on **1.** Pancakes are great for breakfast I could eat them every day.

_____ **2.** Once Carlos saw the painting, he knew he wanted to buy it.

_____ **3.** The animals were restless, they sensed danger was near.

_____ **4.** I hope we can paint the barn before the snow falls.

_____ **5.** Some people believe in UFOs they think people from other planets have visited here.

✏️ _Writing On Your Own_

Each of the following sentences is either a run-on sentence or a comma splice. Rewrite the sentence correctly in the line below using either a semicolon, a period, or a connecting word.

1. Luisa woke up late, she was late for work.

_____

2. The winners were announced Abdul won fifty dollars.

_____

3. Gas rates are high, some families can't afford heat.

_____

4. The cat jumped he landed on the table.

_____

5. We screamed we were very scared.

_____

Rewrite the paragraph in the box. Correct the sentences that are run-ons or comma splices. Do not change the correct sentences.

> If you are a smoker, you have probably noticed more and more "No Smoking" signs. In some cities strict laws have been passed, they forbid smoking in restaurants and offices. Fewer people smoke today everyone knows about the risk of cancer. Maybe someday cigarettes will be a thing of the past.

▲ Looking Back

On the GED Writing Test, some questions ask you to correct **run-on sentences** and **comma splices.** You can prepare by looking over your own writing for sentences that may have gone too far.

Adding Details to Sentences

> *In this lesson you will*
> - write sentences that include details
> - learn to use commas and connecting words correctly when adding details

Picture It

Which of these sentences best describes what is happening in the picture? Mark it with an "X."

_____ **1.** The swimmers cling to the rock.

_____ **2.** The tired and breathless swimmers cling to the rock.

_____ **3.** The tired and breathless swimmers cling desperately to the rock.

_____ **4.** The tired and breathless swimmers cling desperately to the wet, slippery rock.

All the sentences describe the picture. But sentences 2, 3, and 4 each give more **details.** Sentence 4 gives you the most details. It says the swimmers are *tired* and *breathless,* they are feeling *desperate,* and the rock is *wet* and *slippery.*

When you write, you are drawing a picture with words. The reader can more easily "see" the picture when you include descriptive details.

When you add descriptive words to your writing, you often need to use either commas (,) or connecting words like *and, but, or,* and *nor.*

Here's an Example

> You need either a **comma** or a **connecting word** between two details if the phrase still makes sense when you change the order of the details.

Correct: "on a hot, sunny day" OR "on a hot and sunny day"
Why: Since you could *also* say "on a sunny, hot day," you need either a comma or a connecting word.
Incorrect: "on a hot, summer day" OR "on a hot and summer day"
Why: Since you could *not* say "on a summer hot day," you should *not* use either a comma or a connecting word.

> You need either a comma or a connecting word between three or more details. Use a comma if connecting words like *and, or,* and *nor* do *not* join each detail.

Correct: "Michele, Henri, and their children"
Why: Since the word *and* connects only the last two words, you need to put commas after each detail.
Correct: "Michele and Henri and their children"
Why: Since the word *and* connects all three details, commas are not needed.
Incorrect: "Michele, and Henri, and their children"
Why: Since the word *and* connects all three details, commas are not needed.

Working It Out

Decide whether the details given in these sentences need commas. Add the commas where they are needed.

1. The lively graceful dancers leaped around the stage.
2. The angry old woman demanded a refund.
3. The police team worked slowly carefully and skillfully to take apart the bomb.
4. The tired and hungry child cried herself to sleep.
5. My car broke down on a cold windy and snowy evening.

Write a sentence for each group of details given below. The first one is done for you.

1.   quiet   dusty   dark

The dark, dusty, and quiet library was Tom's favorite place.

2.   shiny   red

_____

3.   difficult   new   exciting

_____

4.   out the door   down the path   into the woods

_____

Writing On Your Own

In the first line below each picture, briefly describe the *action* in the picture. Then write at least two descriptive details for each picture. An example is done for you.

kicking a goal
quick
smooth

Now write a sentence that describes each picture. Use the details you listed above. Write three sentences on your own paper.

▲ Looking Back

Would you rather watch television in black and white or in color? Most people prefer color. Sentences with descriptive details are like color television—the action comes across in a livelier, more interesting, and more realistic way.

Adding Descriptive Phrases to Sentences

In this lesson you will
- add descriptive phrases to sentences
- learn how to use commas and connecting words with descriptive phrases

Getting Started

Complete the following survey.

What Are Your Goals?

1. The best thing I have done <u>in the past three years</u> was

_____

2. I would like to be _____

_____ <u>five years from today.</u>

3. I think the most important reason for having a job, <u>not counting</u>

<u>the pay,</u> is _____ .

Would your answers change if the underlined phrases were removed from the survey? Possibly. These descriptive phrases give you extra information to work with. When you write, descriptive phrases will add important details to your sentence.

Here's an Example

Descriptive phrases may explain *why, when, how,* or *where* the action takes place. In the following example, the phrase explains *why* something happens.

■ *To make extra money,* George works the night shift.

Descriptive phrases may come at the beginning, in the middle, or at the end of a sentence. Notice how commas are used.

■ George, *to make extra money,* works the night shift.

■ George works the night shift *to make extra money.*

An Idea to Remember

When a descriptive phrase *starts* the sentence, you usually put a comma after it. When the phrase comes in the *middle* of the sentence, you place commas before and after the phrase only if you hear your voice pause when you read the sentence out loud. When a descriptive phrase *ends* the sentence, you usually do *not* need a comma.

Working It Out

Expand these sentences. Add descriptive words to answer the questions after each sentence. The first one is done for you.

1. Olga wanted to win the race. (Why? How much?)

After losing last year, Olga wanted very much to win the race.

2. Rafael will take the GED exam. (Where? When?)

_____

3. The Gardners are angry. (At whom?)

_____

4. The bus will be late. (Why? When?)

_____

Sometimes you can combine descriptive details from two sentences to make one sentence, as in this example.

■ The lion escaped from its cage. It escaped after the circus performance.

After the circus performance, the lion escaped from its cage.

Combine the descriptive phrases in the following sentence pairs. Make one new sentence. Be sure to use commas correctly.

1. Phyllis and David argued after the concert.
   They argued about their marriage.

   _____

2. Luis quit smoking five years ago.
   He quit smoking after his heart attack.

   _____

3. The Gorskis shop every Saturday.
   They shop at Carter Super Foods.

   _____

Writing On Your Own

Write five sentences using the information in the chart. For each sentence, choose a subject and a verb. Choose two descriptive phrases. Check capitalization, commas, and periods. Use different subjects, verbs, and details for each sentence. You may also add your own details. Use a separate sheet of paper.

Subjects	Descriptive phrases	
the famous actress	to help a friend	after a lot of thought
my son Robert	for the wrong reason as a joke	next month once
I	to stay out of trouble	last summer
the Arnauds	**Verbs**	
	will leave the company robbed a bank want(s) to adopt a child hiked twenty miles	

▲ Looking Back

Descriptive phrases will make your writing more interesting. When you write, use as many details as you can.

Combining Sentences

In this lesson you will

- combine sentences by pairing subjects and verbs
- use connecting words and commas to combine sentences

Getting Started

Read the following letter.

Attention Mrs. Rosalie Steele!

You have six chances to win our Luxury Sweepstakes. Your husband has six chances to win, too. You could win one of our grand prizes. You might drive home in a new car. You might fly to Florida for a seven-day vacation. You might take a cruise to the Bahamas.

To enter the Luxury Sweepstakes, fill out the enclosed entry blank. Sign the entry blank. Return it by midnight on April 1st.

Can you fill in the blanks in this revised letter?

Attention Mrs. Rosalie Steele!

You and _____ each have six chances to win our Luxury Sweepstakes. You could win one of our grand prizes. You might drive home in a new car, or _____ _____ , or _____ .

To enter our Luxury Sweepstakes, fill out the enclosed entry blank. Sign and _____ it by midnight on April 1st.

In the second letter, some of the subjects and verbs from different sentences are combined into one sentence.

Here's an Example

Subjects can be combined if they do the same action. Use **connecting words** like *and, or, either . . . or,* or *neither . . . nor.*

> When you use the connecting word *and,* the subject becomes plural. The verb must **agree** with it.

- Marta wants to go to college someday. Danny wants to go, too. Marta **and** Danny *want* to go to college someday.

Notice how **commas** are used when more than two subjects are combined.

- Marta**,** Danny**, and** Gene want to go to college someday.

Combine the subjects in the following sentences. Use the connecting word *and.*

1. Petra likes to bowl. Jean likes to bowl, too.

_____

2. My dog is hungry. My cat is hungry. My goldfish is hungry.

_____

> When you use the connecting words *or, either . . . or,* or *neither . . . nor* to combine subjects, match the verb to the subject that is closest to it.

- Jane has keys to the car. The boys have keys to the car.
  Either Jane or the boys *have* keys to the car.
  Either the boys or Jane *has* keys to the car.

Combine the subjects in the following sentences. Use the connecting words *either . . . or* or *neither . . . nor.*

3. Ralph will be fired. Judy will be fired.

_____

4. Paco came over. Richard came over.

_____

Verbs can be combined if the subjects are the same and the actions go together. Use connecting words like *and, or, either . . . or,* and *neither . . . nor.*

■ Reuben did not stop at the store. He did not go home.
   Reuben neither stopped at the store nor went home.

Notice how commas are used when more than two verbs are combined.

■ The cowboy rode up to the ranch. He yelled loudly. He threw his hat into the air.
   The cowboy rode up to the ranch, yelled loudly, **and** threw his hat into the air.

Combine the verbs in the following sentences. Use the connecting words *and, or, either . . . or,* or *neither . . . nor.*

5. Roman fixes cars. He builds engines.

_____

6. My aunt watches TV. She plays cards.

_____

Working It Out

Rewrite the following sentence pairs as one complete sentence, combining either the subjects or the verbs. Use the connecting words in parentheses after each sentence. An example is given.

1. The storm damaged four homes. It destroyed many trees. (and)
The storm damaged four homes and destroyed many trees.

2. Anne danced with Kevin. Beth danced with Kevin. (either . . . or)

_____

3. Leroy does not sing. The Grants don't either. (neither . . . nor)

_____

4. The dog wagged her tail. She barked at me. (and)

_____

5. Mark could have come earlier. Jay could have come earlier. (or)

_____

6. Tony called his mother. He went to see her. (either . . . or)

_____

7. Mrs. Johnson left her house. She walked to the car. (and)

_____

8. Jane is tired. The children are tired. (or)

_____

9. I drove a truck. I operated a crane. (and)

_____

10. We'll have a party. We'll go to the shore. (either . . . or)

_____

11. The baby does not walk. The baby does not talk. (or)

_____

12. The bus goes there. The train goes there. (and)

_____

13. The bank was not open. The post office was not open. (neither . . . nor)

_____

✏️ Writing On Your Own

Read the following paragraph. Decide which subjects and verbs can be combined. Rewrite the paragraph on your own paper.

■ People have different opinions about hair. Movie stars spend lots of money to find the right hairstyle. So do teenagers. However, some people don't worry about hair. They may keep it very short. They may let it grow out long. They may even shave it off completely.

▲ Looking Back

After you write a paragraph, go back later and ask yourself, "Can any of these sentences be combined?" Then rewrite the sentences that can be combined.

Combining Complete Thoughts

> *In this lesson you will*
> - learn ways to combine ideas using commas and connecting words

Picture It

Read the following story. Fill in each blank with a connecting word from the box in the margin.

- I heard where the bomb was planted, _____ I knew what time the plane to Paris would leave. It seemed impossible to stop the terrorists, _____ I had to try. I jumped into my car, _____ it wouldn't start. I had very little time, _____ I leaped into the nearest taxi. I had to reach the airport by six, _____ the plane would blow up!

yet	or
and	so
but	

In earlier lessons, you read about complete, independent thoughts—ideas that can stand alone. In each sentence above, two complete thoughts were joined together using a comma and a connecting word. The connecting word shows *how* the two ideas go together.

Complete thoughts can go together in four different ways:

1. You can add one idea to another.

2. You can contrast two ideas, showing how they are different.

3. You can show how one idea causes another.

4. You can show how two ideas are two different choices.

Here's an Example

> **1.** When one idea is added to another, use a comma and the connecting word *and*.

Example: I heard where the bomb was planted, **and** I knew what time the plane to Paris would leave.

> **2.** If one idea contrasts with another, use a comma and the word *yet* or *but*.

Example: It seemed impossible to stop the terrorists, **yet** I had to try. I jumped into my car, **but** it wouldn't start.

> **3.** When the first idea causes the second, use a comma and the word *so*.

Example: I had very little time, **so** I leaped into the nearest taxi.

> **4.** If the two ideas are different choices or possibilities, use a comma and the word *or*.

Example: I had to reach the airport by six, **or** the plane would blow up!

Working It Out

Fill in a connecting word to complete each sentence below.

1. Jon is coming over, _____ he's bringing Janet.

2. Mary wants to come, _____ she might have to work.

3. Willie gets off at ten, _____ he'll be a little late.

4. Eva had better hurry, _____ she won't make it on time.

5. Everyone will bring something, _____ we don't have to cook.

Combine the following sentence pairs using a comma and a connecting word. The first one is done for you.

1. Randy is in the hospital. He can't go to the conference.

Randy is in the hospital, so he can't go to the conference.

2. Lisa is on another diet. She still eats ice cream sundaes.

_____

3. Amy will borrow money. Otherwise she'll have to go home.

_____

4. Hector changed jobs last month. Now his wife has a new job.

_____

5. Dogs are smart animals. Pigs are even smarter.

_____

Writing On Your Own

Complete the following sentences by adding a comma, a connecting word, and another complete thought.
An example is given.

1. In the middle of the party we ran out of ice ___*, so I* _____ *went to the store to buy more.*

2. The weather report promised sunny skies for Saturday _____

_____

3. Senator Dawson barely won the last election _____

_____

4. Smoke was pouring out from under the hood of the car _____

_____

5. Cathy has had problems with her boss _____

_____

▲ Looking Back

When you combine two ideas in a sentence, use connecting words to show how the two ideas *go together*.

Combining Unequal Ideas

In this lesson you will
- learn to use commas and connecting words to combine unequal ideas

Picture It

Sometimes you'll write two ideas that are not of equal importance. One is the main idea. The other is a secondary idea. Here's how to put them together.

Look at the three pictures below. See if you can fill in the blanks under the third picture.

Annette was balancing a tray of drinks.

Louise stood up suddenly.

While Annette _____

_____ ,

Louise _____

_____ .

The first picture expresses an independent thought—"Annette was balancing a tray of drinks." The second picture also shows an independent thought—"Louise stood up suddenly." But the third picture puts the two ideas together. It shows us a dependent thought ("While Annette was balancing a tray of drinks") and an independent thought ("Louise stood up suddenly.")

If you wrote only, "While Annette was balancing a tray of drinks," someone might ask, "What happened?" This part of the sentence depends on the main idea, "Louise stood up suddenly."

Here's an Example

Read the following phrases.

When Chris called . . .   . . . **because** it's mine.
If we can't go . . .   . . . **until** Kurt returns.

Each phrase is an example of a dependent thought, a thought that can't stand alone.

Here are some of the **connecting words** that join dependent thoughts to the main idea.

after	by the time	since	whenever
although	even though	though	where
as long as	if	unless	wherever
because	just as	until	whether
before	once	when	while

> If a dependent thought *begins* a sentence, it is followed by a comma. If a dependent thought *ends* the sentence, you usually don't need a comma.

Incorrect: When the game was over everyone left the stadium.
  Correct: When the game was over, everyone left the stadium.
  Correct: Everyone left the stadium when the game was over.

Now it's your turn. Find two ways to rewrite the sentence below.
Incorrect: If you want to stay we can stay.

1. Correct: _____

2. Correct: _____

> Different connecting words give different meanings to a sentence.

See how the meaning of each sentence changes when the connecting word is changed.

- Because Aunt Mabel liked Jimmy, she scolded him.
  Although Aunt Mabel liked Jimmy, she scolded him.

The first sentence says that the *reason* Aunt Mabel scolded Jimmy was *because* she liked him. The second sentence says that Aunt Mabel scolded Jimmy *although* she liked him. See the difference?

- When Alice finishes the bedroom, she will paint the bathroom.
  If Alice finishes the bedroom, she will paint the bathroom.

The first sentence gives the idea that Alice will *definitely* finish the bedroom. The second sentence says that *maybe* Alice will finish the bedroom.

Use two different connecting words to combine the following sentences.

- You have a good reason. I won't let you leave early.

1. _____

2. _____

Working It Out

Combine the sentence pairs below into a new sentence with a dependent thought and an independent thought. Remember to add a connecting word and to use a comma if necessary. An example is given.

1. Paul did his homework. He listened to music.

While Paul did his homework, he listened to music.

2. Cynthia is tired. She'll work late.

_____

3. Shelley calls about the movie. We'll decide if we're going.

_____

4. Jan will finish the project. Ahmed doesn't have time.

_____

5. The rain stopped. The sun came out.

_____

6. Sally can afford a vacation. She got her tax refund.

_____

✏️ Writing On Your Own

Complete the sentences by adding either an independent thought or a dependent thought. An example is given.

1. By the time Amelia called the doctor, _she was feeling dizzy and weak_.

2. Barry drove home slowly _____

_____

3. Even though we were scared, _____

_____

4. This trail will be easier to follow _____

_____

5. After Maria's visit, _____

_____

6. Chris will get a new job _____

_____

7. When Mary won the lottery, _____

_____

8. I asked him to look at my car _____

_____

9. My wife always gets mad _____

_____

10. Just as Mr. Ramos pulled into his driveway, _____

_____

▲ Looking Back

Combining ideas will make your writing stronger. You'll be able to show clearly how your ideas go together.

Taking Notes

In this lesson you will

- learn how good note-taking will improve your writing
- learn how to take notes on articles and talks

Getting Started

Imagine that you live in the city of Fremont. Read the following article.

Fremont May Get New Freeway

The City Council today said it will "consider" plans to build a new freeway. The road would connect the southeast and northwest sides of Fremont. Work could begin as early as next summer.

Spokesperson Brenda Barker said the City Council "wants to cut down on traffic jams." She said a new freeway "might be the answer."

The new freeway would pass through the neighborhoods of Harter Heights and Greenview. About seven hundred homes would have to be torn down.

Councilman Nick Picone is against the new freeway. His district includes Harter Heights and Greenview. In fact, his own home will be torn down if the new freeway is built. He plans to fight the new freeway.

You live in Harter Heights. Your home could be torn down. What will you do? Call the mayor's office? Write a letter to the City Council? Organize a meeting of people in your neighborhood?

Before you do anything, you must first make sure you *understand* and *remember* the facts. You can keep track of important facts by taking notes.

You can take notes on something you *read,* such as a newspaper article, or something you *hear,* such as a speech. When you take notes, you write down the most important details. You decide which facts you want to remember.

Here's an Example

The following is an example of notes you could take on the newspaper article. Can you finish the notes by filling in the blanks?

1	*"Fremont May Get New Freeway"*	*Fremont Press 11/8*
2		
3	*City Council may build new freeway*	
4	*— would connect SE + NW Fremont*	
5	*— could be started* _____	
6	*Council wants to* _____	
7	*Freeway to go through* _____	
8	*— about 700 homes to be torn down*	
9	*Nick Picone is* _____	
10	*— his district is Harter Hgts. + Greenview*	
11	*— his home would be torn down*	

Tips for Good Note-Taking

- Read the article once before taking notes.
- Write down the name of the article, the magazine or newspaper where you found it, and the date. (**Example:** line 1)
- Look for the main ideas. Don't include unimportant details. (**Example:** line 3)
- Write down short phrases and sentences. Don't worry about grammar or punctuation. (**Example:** line 8)
- Use abbreviations you can remember later. (**Example:** line 4)
- Use a new line for each new idea. You can indent details underneath the main idea. (**Example:** lines 4–5)
- Later, review your notes. Underline or highlight the key words and phrases. (**Example:** lines 3, 7, 9)

Working It Out

Imagine you heard a speech by Nick Picone. He was explaining why he is against the new freeway. Complete the notes below by adding the important details of his talk.

"Ladies and gentlemen, I am against the new freeway, for three very good reasons.

"First, Fremont is not getting any bigger. Since 1990, our population has stayed close to half a million. In the future we're more likely to get smaller, not bigger. Fremont doesn't need any more roads because we won't have more cars.

"Second, local business would suffer. If we build that freeway, we would make it easier for people to drive out to the malls. Meanwhile, here in Fremont our stores would lose customers. That would not be good for anyone.

"Third, Fremont is a city with character. We're not New York or Los Angeles, and we don't want to be. We don't tear down someone's home just so we can move faster from one place to another. Life moves slower here in Fremont. We should be proud of that. In conclusion, I say that Fremont doesn't need another freeway."

Nick Picone — November 10th — Hull Library, 8:00 P.M.
Against freeway for 3 reasons:
① Fremont isn't growing — still 1/2 million since '90
— no need for more roads
② Bad for local businesses —
③
Conclusion:

Here are some hints for taking notes of a talk:

■ Start writing as soon as the speaker begins.
■ Listen for main ideas. Don't try to write down everything the speaker says.
■ Sometimes a speaker will help you by using key phrases like "There are **two** reasons . . . ," or, "I have **five** major

points . . . ." When you hear that, write down "2 reasons" or "5 points." Then as the speaker gives each point, write it down and number it.

Writing On Your Own

Imagine you want to write a letter to the City Council to argue against the new freeway. Read the following article. In the space below, write notes of the important ideas you would want to include in your letter.

Fremont Press   November 25, 1994

New Study Says Freeway Isn't Needed

A study done by Fremont County says that a new freeway may not be needed to solve Fremont's traffic problems.

The study looks at Riverfront Drive, Fremont's busiest street. The study says that changes in parking zones, stop signs, and traffic signals would solve the traffic jams.

The new freeway would cost $100 million. The study says the cost of fixing Riverfront Drive and other roads would only be about $4 million.

Traffic jams can be taken care of without building a new freeway, the study concluded.

| |
| |
| |
| |
| |
| |
| |
| |
| |

▲ Looking Back

Compare your notes with the checklist on page 84. Did you include all the important facts? Did you follow the steps for good note-taking?

When you need information for your writing, taking notes will help you pull everything together.

Outlining

In this lesson you will
- learn how to write an outline

Picture It

Look at the groceries in the picture. Where would you store each item? Write your answers under each heading below.

Refrigerator	Freezer	Kitchen Cupboard	Bathroom Closet
_____	_____	_____	_____
_____	_____	_____	_____

At your home, you probably don't put ice cream in the bathroom closet or soap in the refrigerator. Your home is organized so that you can find things and use them.

You can organize information too. Then you can easily find it and use it in your writing. One way to organize information is by outlining. When you make an **outline,** you show how different details are related to a main topic.

Here's an Example

With three children and a job, Lucy was going crazy trying to do a hundred things in a day. "I have to get my life organized!" she said. She wrote this outline of her daily routine. Can you fill in the blanks with the phrases in the box?

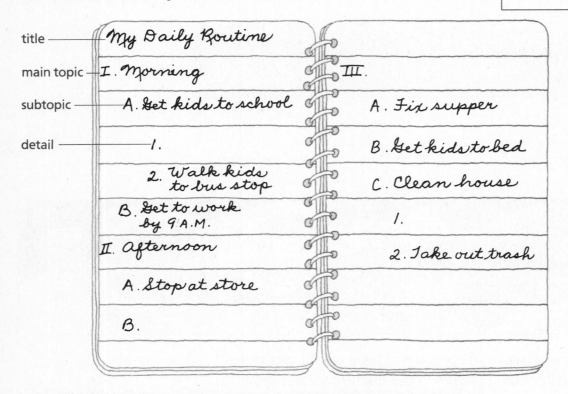

title ——
main topic ——
subtopic ——
detail ——

My Daily Routine

I. Morning

   A. Get kids to school

      1.

      2. Walk kids
         to bus stop

   B. Get to work
      by 9 A.M.

II. Afternoon

   A. Stop at store

   B.

III.

   A. Fix supper

   B. Get kids to bed

   C. Clean house

      1.

      2. Take out trash

Parts of an Outline

1. The **title.** The title comes first. It explains what the outline is about.
2. The **main topics.** The main topics give the most important ideas.
3. The **subtopics.** Every main topic may have some subtopics. The subtopics give more information about the main topic.
4. The **details.** Every subtopic may have some details underneath it. The details give more information about the subtopic.

Subtopics and details are indented a few spaces under the main topics.

Working It Out

Lucy organized her day by making an outline. In the same way, you can see how an article is organized by outlining it.

Here is the beginning of an article on test-taking tips. Read the article. Then complete the outline below it.

Test-Taking Tips

Do you get nervous when you have to take a test? Many people do. Here is some advice on what to do before and during a test.

Before you take a test, it's important to do two things: *study* and *relax.* When you study for a test, take notes on the important points. Read your notes carefully. Make up questions that could be on the test. Try to answer your questions.

When you study, do a little at a time. Don't try to learn everything at the last minute. Instead, study for an hour or two every day.

After you study, relax! Take fifteen minutes after each study session to exercise or stretch. While you're relaxing, *think positive.* Tell yourself, "I am going to do well on this test."

Fill in the blanks to complete this outline.

Test-Taking Tips

I. Before the test

  A. Study

    1. Take notes on important points

    2. _____

    3. _____

  B. _____

    1. Exercise or stretch

    2. _____

Writing On Your Own

Now you will make your own outline. Read the rest of the article on taking a test. In the lines that follow it, outline the information in the article.

During the test, remember these points. First, have everything you need close by. Bring extra pencils or pens and keep them on the desk. If there is an answer sheet, keep the answer sheet next to the test.

Second, keep track of time. As you go through the test, don't spend too much time on the hard questions. Instead, do all the questions you know first. Then go back and work on the hard ones.

Finally, check your work. Go over all your answers. Make sure your answers match up to the right questions. If you skipped any, try to answer them now. Don't turn your test in early—use all the time you have to check your work.

Write your outline here. The first line is done for you.

II. During the test _____

_____

_____

_____

_____

_____

_____

_____

_____

_____

▲ Looking Back

When you outline an article, you can see how it's organized and understand it better. That makes it easier to write about.

Writing a Summary

> *In this lesson you will*
> ■ learn to write a summary

Getting Started

In the last two lessons you learned to take notes and outline. One more skill will also help you understand what you read: **summarizing.** Read the following article.

Sojourner Truth: Fighting for Freedom

1   More than one hundred years ago, a poor African American woman was fighting for the rights of women and African Americans. Her name was Sojourner Truth.

2   Sojourner was born a slave in the late 1700s. She was freed in 1817. When she heard her son was still a slave, she took his owner to court. She told the judge that her son should be free. The judge agreed with her, and her son was freed.

3   Everyone was shocked. No one thought a poor African American woman could win a legal case against a white man.

4   Sojourner kept fighting against slavery. In the years before the Civil War, she traveled all over the northern states. She preached for the freedom of all people.

5   Sojourner also fought for women's rights. In 1851, she went to the Woman's Rights Convention in Akron, Ohio. She heard a minister say that women were too weak to vote.

6   Then Sojourner asked to speak. In a loud voice she told everyone that she had plowed fields, lifted heavy loads, and even been whipped. As she spoke of each hardship she asked the crowd, "And ain't I a woman?" She made people realize how strong a woman could be.

7   Today, Sojourner Truth is still remembered for her brave fight against racism and sexism.

In this lesson you will summarize the information about Sojourner Truth.

When you state the main idea of a paragraph, article, or story, leaving out all the less important details, you are **summarizing**. Summarizing what you read will help you understand it better.

Here's an Example

Circle the letter next to the sentence that is a good summary of paragraph 2.
   A. Sojourner heard her son was still a slave.
   B. Sojourner was born a slave, but was freed in 1817.
   C. After she was freed from slavery, Sojourner went to court and won her son's freedom.

You should have circled C. This is a good summary because it gives the most important information in the paragraph.

Working It Out

1. The following phrases are details from paragraph 6. Which detail should *not* be included in a summary? Cross it out.
   A. she made people realize a woman could be strong
   B. she spoke in a loud voice
   C. she spoke at the Woman's Rights Convention
   D. she had worked very hard
2. Explain **why** the detail you crossed out in question 1 does not belong in a summary.

_____

3. Write a one-sentence **summary** of paragraph 4 in the article.

_____

_____

_____

An Idea to Remember

A summary is a short statement—no more than a few sentences. It gives only the author's main ideas, not the details.

4. Which of the following paragraphs is the best summary of the whole article? Circle the correct letter.

A. Sojourner Truth was born in the late 1700s. She was a poor African American woman. She traveled all over the North. She went to the Woman's Rights Convention in Ohio and spoke to people in a loud voice. She said she had plowed fields. She is still remembered today.

B. Sojourner Truth fought for equal rights for women and African Americans. After she was freed from slavery, Sojourner went to court and won her son's freedom. In 1851, she went to the Woman's Rights Convention in Ohio. She showed people that women could be strong by telling about the hard things she had done in her life. Today, her work has not been forgotten.

C. Sojourner Truth went to court to fight for her son's freedom. Then she went to the Woman's Rights Convention in Akron, Ohio. She heard a minister say that women were too weak to vote. Then Sojourner asked to speak. Her words against racism are still remembered today.

Writing On Your Own

For this section, you will need to look back at the article "Test-Taking Tips" on page 89–90.

Write a summary of the whole article. (**Hint:** Your outline on pages 89 and 90 will help you find the most important points.)

_____

_____

_____

_____

_____

▲ Looking Back

Summarizing will help you understand what you read. The better you understand something, the easier it is to write about. When you have all the facts together, the job of writing about them is much easier!

Fine-Tuning Your Writing

In this lesson you will
- learn how to spell and use some confusing words
- learn how to use contractions and possessives that sound the same
- learn more about subject-verb agreement

Getting Started

In the past lessons you've written quite a lot. Now it's time to fine-tune your writing. In this lesson you will look at a few small details that can make a big difference in your written work.

Here's a short quiz. You can use it to see which of these details you already know. Read each sentence. If the underlined word is correct as written, write ''correct'' in the blank. If it is incorrect, write the correct word in the blank.

_____ 1. I can't <u>except</u> what you're saying.

_____ 2. <u>Their</u> going to the beach tomorrow.

_____ 3. The picture with wildflowers <u>are</u> my favorite.

_____ 4. Sally walked slowly through the <u>quite</u> rooms.

_____ 5. <u>It's</u> hard to say how Alex is feeling.

_____ 6. Nancy, together with the BoMonts, <u>is</u> singing tonight.

Check your answers on page 247. How did you do? The next sections will show you how to handle these three writing details:
- confusing word sets
- contractions and possessives
- interrupting phrases

Here's an Example
Confusing Word Sets

Here are six sets of words that often confuse writers.

accept-except   loose-lose   to-too-two
choose-chose   quiet-quite

See the correct use of each word in the sentences below.

- The union members **accept** the contract, **except** for the rule on overtime pay.
  accept–to take or permit
  except–other than, but

- Greg **chose** a black sweater, but Audrey will **choose** a green one.
  chose–past time form of *choose*
  choose–to select

- If the horse's rope is **loose,** we may **lose** him.
  loose–not tight
  lose–to fail to keep

- The children are **quiet** because they are **quite** tired.
  quiet– not making noise
  quite– very

- The **two** of you are **too** angry **to** think clearly.
  two–the number following *one*
  too–more than enough, or also
  to–a connecting word

Working It Out

Read each sentence and decide if the underlined word is used correctly. If it is, write "correct" in the blank. If it is not, write the correct word in the blank.

_____ 1. Martin is afraid he will <u>loose</u> his job.

_____ 2. Vicky is <u>quiet</u> sure of herself.

_____ 3. The judges <u>chose</u> a winner yesterday.

_____ 4. My cat has <u>too</u> stop scratching people.

_____ 5. Karen feels fine, <u>except</u> for a slight headache.

_____ 6. You can't have <u>two</u> many friends.

Here's an Example

Contractions and Possessives

A contraction combines two words into one, using an **apostrophe** ('). Here are some examples of contractions. Can you fill in the blanks?

do not → don't   she will → she'll   it is → _____

you are → you're   were not → _____   will not → won't

A possessive pronoun shows ownership. Pronouns that don't refer to a particular person or thing — such as *someone, everybody,* and *one* — add *'s* to become possessive. No other pronouns use an apostrophe to become possessive. Look at the following:

their balloon   **its** leash   Is this **hers**?

someone's idea   **whose** money   **nobody's** business

Some contractions and possessive pronouns sound the same but are written differently. Writers often get these words confused.

Contraction:	they're	there's	it's	who's	you're
Possessive:	their	theirs	its	whose	your

When you want to use one of these words in a sentence, ask:
- Can I write it as two words? **Use the contraction.**
- Does it show ownership? **Use the possessive.**

Working It Out

Underline the correct word in each of the following sentences.

1. (Their/They're) not very friendly to anyone.

2. (Whose/Who's) making dinner tonight?

3. (Its/It's) feathers are coming out.

4. Karen knows (your/you're) mother quite well.

5. Jasper believes (theirs/there's) no reason to vote.

6. If (your/you're) not satisfied, let us know.

7. (Its/It's) probably going to snow tonight.

Rewrite each sentence correctly.

8. Who's phone number is written in you're notebook?

---

9. It's the number of my new neighbors. Their next door to me.

___

10. If its theirs, tell me why theirs a heart drawn around it!

___

Here's an Example
Interrupting Phrases

An **interrupting phrase** is a phrase that comes between a subject and a verb. When a noun is part of an interrupting phrase, writers sometimes think it is the subject. They make the verb agree with the noun in the interrupting phrase. Here's what that mistake looks like.

Incorrect: My favorite part of baseball games **are** the seventh-inning stretch.

Why: The subject is *part,* not *games,* so the verb must agree with *part.* Instead, it agrees with *games.*

Correct: My favorite **part** of baseball games **is** the seventh-inning stretch.

There is a difference between a sentence with a subject and an interrupting phrase, and a sentence with combined subjects. As you learned in Lesson 19, if two subjects are combined with the connecting word *and,* the verb is plural.

Correct: Carol and her three sisters plan to be doctors.

Why: The subjects are *Carol* and *her three sisters,* so the verb must agree with a plural subject.

Working It Out

Underline the correct verb in each of the following sentences.

1. The Christmas trees, each crowned with a star, (was/were) beautiful.
2. George Kramer, like many other teachers, (enjoys/enjoy) having the summer off.
3. This new cake mix with real walnuts (is/are) delicious.
4. Jacob and Frieda (loves/love) to give gifts.
5. The day after final exams (is/are) the time to relax.

Rewrite the following sentences correctly.

6. I, like my father, loves a clean home.

___

7. My son and I doesn't agree about cleaning.

_____

8. He, like all his friends, clean house about once a year.

_____

9. He and his friends says it just gets dirty again anyway.

_____

⟹ Writing On Your Own

The following paragraph has a number of errors like the ones you have just studied. Rewrite the paragraph below, correcting each error.

■ Some people say that patience is a virtue, but I think their wrong. Its too easy to wait around until something good happens. I believe that life is you're responsibility. Sometimes you, like everyone else, has to make things change. You can chose to do nothing or too take action. You won't win every time, but you will learn something even when you loose.

_____
_____
_____
_____
_____
_____
_____
_____
_____

▲ Looking Back

When you fine-tune a radio, the message comes in more sharply and clearly. When you fine-tune your sentences by paying attention to details, the reader will have a sharper, clearer understanding of your writing.

Revising and Editing

> **In this lesson you will**
> - learn tips for revising and editing your writing
> - practice revising and editing your own work

Getting Started

You have learned how to write sharp, clear sentences in the other lessons in this book. You've learned some tips for good writing. Now it's time to put everything together.

A **checklist** can help you take a step-by-step look at your writing. You can use a checklist to help you revise and edit your sentences.

When you **revise** sentences, you make sure your ideas are clear. You look at the words you've used. Are they the best words to say what you mean? You add details. You make your sentences more interesting and effective.

Here is a checklist you can use to help you revise. Use it to help make your writing better. If you need extra help, turn back to the lessons listed after each question.

Revising Checklist
- Have you given enough information? (See Lesson 1.)
- Is your topic clear? (See Lesson 2.)
- Have you given descriptive details? (See Lessons 5—8, 18, and 19.)
- Have you used active, concrete verbs? (See Lesson 13.)
- Can any phrases or sentences be combined? (See Lessons 19—22.)

When you **edit** sentences, you check for mistakes in spelling, grammar, and punctuation. Everyone makes mistakes. So it helps to look over your sentences one last time with these questions in mind.

Editing Checklist

- Is your handwriting easy to read? (See Lesson 3.)
- Are words spelled correctly? (See Lessons 6 and 26.)
- Are words capitalized correctly? (See Lessons 9 and 14.)
- Do the pronouns agree with the nouns and other pronouns they replace? (See Lesson 10.)
- Do the verbs agree with their subjects? (See Lessons 11 and 20.)
- Are all verbs written in the correct verb time? (See Lesson 12.)
- Is each sentence a complete sentence? (See Lessons 16 and 17.)
- Does each sentence end with a period, question mark, or exclamation point? (See Lessons 14 and 15.)
- Are commas and connecting words used correctly? (See Lessons 17–22 and 26.)

Here's an Example

Jamie wrote these sentences describing her new job. She wrote down all her ideas without worrying about mistakes.

- I work on factery line to put radios in boxes. Not hard work, but sometimes boring. now I get payed vacation

Jamie knew she still had to revise and edit what she had written. Here is how she **revised** her sentences.

I work on factery line ~~to put~~ radios in boxes. ~~Not hard work~~,
but sometimes boring. now I get payed vacation

Next Jamie **edited** her sentences.

I work on a factory line packing radios in boxes. The work isn't hard but sometimes its boring. now though I get payed vacation .

Her final copy looked like this.

- I work on a factory line packing radios in boxes. The work isn't hard, but sometimes it's boring. Now, though, I get paid vacation.

An Idea to Remember

You can make your **revising** changes right on the first copy you wrote. Then write out your revised sentences. Make your **editing** changes on that copy. Finally, write out a clean copy in your best handwriting. If you're like most writers, you'll have to write your sentences out a few times before you're happy with them.

Working It Out

Read the following sentences. Use the **Revising Checklist** to revise each sentence. Rewrite the revised sentences on the lines below.

- Drugs can save lives. Drugs can take lives. They can be good. They can be bad. It depends on how they are used by people.

_____

_____

_____

_____

Now read these sentences. Use the **Editing Checklist** to edit each sentence. Rewrite the edited sentences on the lines below.

- The town of White River seen it's first soccer match last thursday. Our new soccer team the White River Rockets beat the Lincoln City pirates. The score were 3–1.

_____

_____

_____

_____

✏️ Writing On Your Own

On this page, write a few sentences describing your favorite place to be. Explain where it is, what it looks like, who is there, and why you like to be there. Don't worry about grammar, spelling, or punctuation—just write down your thoughts as they come out. If you want more room to write, do this assignment on a separate sheet of paper.

_____

_____

_____

_____

_____

Finished? Now you are going to revise your writing. Use the **Revising Checklist** to help you make changes. Rewrite your revised sentences on the lines below.

_____

_____

_____

_____

Here is the last step—editing your sentences. Use the **Editing Checklist** to check every detail. Make your corrections. Then rewrite your edited sentences on the lines below.

_____

_____

_____

_____

▲ Looking Back

Revising and editing make writing easier! When you begin to write, you can concentrate on writing down all your thoughts. You know you'll catch any mistakes later on.

Measuring What You've Learned

This section will help you see how much you've learned so far in this book. Complete each part carefully.

A. Rewrite the following sentence, changing from informal to formal language.

1. The window that's broke is no big deal.

_____

B. Identify the topic of the following paragraph.

■ There are many ways to buy vegetables. You can buy frozen, canned, or fresh vegetables. Fresh vegetables are considered the most healthy.

2. TOPIC: _____

C. Use context clues to choose the correct word in each sentence. Underline your answer.

3. Keith may (loose/lose) all his friends.
4. (Its/It's) hard to cross the river right now.
5. I had (quite/quiet) a good time last night.
6. (Your/You're) homework is missing.

D. If you looked up these words in a dictionary, which words would be on the page with these guide words: picture *and* poison? *Underline your answers.*

7. period   pleasant   pocket   paid   piece   police

E. Add the correct capitalization and punctuation to the following sentences.

8. did martha go to arizona last winter
9. redbud park opens for camping every may

F. In each sentence below, pronouns are used incorrectly. Rewrite each sentence correctly.

10. You shouldn't judge others without looking at oneself.

_____

11. The puppy has their eyes open already.

_____

G. Underline the correct verb in each of the following sentences.

12. We (doesn't/don't) want to move.

13. He (be/is) thinking about work all the time.

14. The flowers (are/were) picked yesterday.

15. Larry (saw/seen) a fight in the alley.

16. I (hope/hopes) John calls soon.

H. Rewrite the following sentences replacing each verb with an active, concrete verb.

17. Judy was told the news by her boss.

_____

18. The rabbit went through the bushes.

_____

I. Decide whether each of the following sentences is a statement, a question, a command, or an exclamation. Write ''statement,'' ''question,'' ''command,'' or ''exclamation'' in the blank.

_____ **19.** What a wonderful morning this is!

_____ **20.** Get me more information.

_____ **21.** Are there any cookies left?

J. Read each of the following examples. If it is a complete sentence, write "complete" in the blank. If it is a run-on sentence, write "run-on." If it is a comma splice, write "comma splice." If it is a sentence fragment, write "fragment."

_____ **22.** After the rain stopped, the air smelled fresh.

_____ **23.** The last time Gary was here.

_____ **24.** Al walked to work, he missed the bus.

_____ **25.** Time flies.

_____ **26.** Sara spoke next she talked about Italy.

_____ **27.** The wind howled the thunder roared.

K. Combine details in these sentence pairs to make one sentence.

28. Milo was tired. He was hungry.

_____

29. The bear watched the deer. It was a large, powerful bear.

_____

L. Combine either the subjects or the verbs in these sentence pairs to make one sentence.

30. Jacques called me. He talked about his girlfriend.

_____

31. Alice believes in astrology. Vanessa does, too.

_____

M. Use the words in parentheses to combine the following sentence pairs into one sentence. Watch your punctuation.

32. Melinda wants to buy a car. She can't afford it. (but)

_____

33. We were on vacation. Someone broke into our house. (while)

_____

34. Don't park here. You could get a ticket. (or)

_____

35. Raissa loves pea soup. She won't eat peas. (even though)

_____

N. Read the following article.

The Moscow Metro
The busiest subway in the world is in the city of Moscow, the capital of Russia. Each day 3.5 million people travel on the Metro, as the subway is called.

The Metro has 70 stations and more than 250 miles of track. For tourists and commuters, the Metro is a good way to get around the city.

The Moscow subway is also famous for its art. Paintings and sculptures by top Russian artists are found in many Metro stations. A subway may seem like a strange place to show art, but think of how many people see it!

36. If you made an outline of this article, which three phrases could be your three main topics? Underline them.

world's busiest subway   3.5 million people   a good way to travel

for tourists and commuters   famous for its art   Russian artists

37. Write a summary of the article.

_____

_____

_____

38. The following paragraph has many mistakes. Edit the paragraph and rewrite a correct version on your own paper.

■ Its not easy too learn another language? No matter where your from, your own language always seem more simple than a language one doesn't know. children often had fewer problems. Since their able to copy many sounds. Whether the language is spanish japanese or Greek, children can often learn them faster than adults.

You can check your answers on pages 248–249.

Your Results

How did you do? Did you miss any questions? The following table tells you which lessons you can review for each question you missed.

If you missed question:	Review lesson:
1	1
2	2
3, 4, 5, 6	5, 26
7	6
8, 9	9, 14, 15
10, 11	10
12, 13, 14, 15, 16	11, 12
17, 18	13
19, 20, 21	15
22, 23, 24, 25, 26, 27	16, 17
28, 29	18, 19
30, 31	20
32, 33, 34, 35	21, 22
36	24
37	25
38	27

Part B
Writing Paragraphs

In **Part B,** you will build skills in writing paragraphs. You'll learn how to get ideas for writing. You'll learn how to organize ideas. You'll practice writing a first draft. And you'll learn how to go back over your paragraph to improve it.

You write for many different reasons. In these lessons, you'll learn how to write paragraphs for all those reasons. Each time you write a new paragraph, you'll go through the same process. You'll collect and organize ideas. You'll find your main idea. You'll write a first draft. You'll revise and edit what you've written.

These lessons will give you practice in writing. You'll find that the more writing you do, the better your writing will become. Writing a good paragraph is the first step in writing a good essay. The skills you learn in this book will help you as you go on to prepare for the GED Writing Test.

Measuring What You Know

This survey will help you find out how well you write. It asks you to write on three different topics.

1. Write about yourself. Tell what you do at home, at work, or at your adult class. Use scratch paper if you like. You should write about five sentences. Then write your best copy on the lines below.

_____

_____

_____

_____

_____

_____

2. Write about a person you like. Tell why you like this person. You should write about five sentences. Use scratch paper if you like. Then write your best copy on the lines below.

_____

_____

_____

_____

_____

_____

3. Write about five sentences telling your feelings about divorce. Tell why divorce is good or bad for a person. Use scratch paper if you like. Then write your best copy on the lines below.

_____

_____

_____

_____

_____

_____

Your Results

Now that you've written on three topics, ask your teacher to score your writing.

How did you do on the Writing Survey? Your scores show what skills you're good at. They also show what skills you need to work on when you study this book.

Now you are ready to start improving your writing skills.

Prewriting Activities

Your Purpose and Your Audience

> **In this lesson you will**
> - read about the reasons people write
> - learn about writing for a particular reader

Picture It

Have you ever read an ad in the classified section of the newspaper? A classified ad has just a few words. One of the ads could look like this:

The thirty-year-old woman had a reason for writing this ad. She wants to get a baby-sitting job. She's trying to get someone to hire her. That is her purpose — to persuade someone.

> **An Idea to Remember**
>
> **Purpose** is the reason a person writes something. The main reasons people write are:
> 1. *to tell* about something that happened
> 2. *to describe* something
> 3. *to explain* how or why something is done
> 4. *to persuade* someone to think or act in a certain way

The woman hopes that someone looking for a baby-sitter will read her ad. People who need a baby-sitter make up the woman's audience. An **audience** is the person or group of people who read a piece of writing.

When you write, you need to think about your purpose for writing. You also need to know who your audience will be.

Here's an Example

Suppose you want to write about your car. Ask yourself, *"Why do I want to write about my car?"* You decide you want to describe it. That is your purpose—to describe your car.

To describe means to give a picture in words. You'll want to include details that give a picture of the car, such as these:

red body   white top   roomy   350 engine

white inside , cloth seats   4 doors   radial tires

To figure out your audience, think, "Who will read my description of the car?" Say you want to describe it to your ten-year-old nephew. A ten-year-old will want to know the colors. He may want to know that the car is big and has cloth seats. He probably won't care about the engine size or tires.

Can you see how your purpose (to describe your car) and your audience (your nephew) will affect what you write?

Working It Out

Purpose: The main purposes in writing are *to tell about an event, to describe, to explain,* and *to persuade.* Each of the sentences below is from a piece of writing. Which purpose do you think the writer had in each piece?

1. The house was the most beautiful one I had ever seen.

Purpose: _____

2. No one should drink and then drive.

Purpose: _____

3. This computer is easy to use.

Purpose: _____

4. Last Saturday night started out quietly.

Purpose: _____

Audience: Below is a list of people. Put each one next to the subject he or she probably would *most* like to read about.

retired worker   doctor   teacher   mother   athlete

minister   child   driver   cook   teenager

1. recipes _____
2. hospitals _____
3. churches _____
4. rock music _____
5. speed limits _____

6. new toys _____
7. math books _____
8. gym shoes _____
9. leisure time _____
10. family fun _____

Read the pieces of writing below. Tell what you think is the writer's purpose (tell about an event, describe, explain, or persuade). Then write who you think the writer's audience is.

Memo: The lunchroom is the only place where smoking will be allowed in this building.

Purpose: _____   Audience: _____

Vote! Vote for Jim Bills in Tuesday's election. He will build housing for the older people in town.

Purpose: _____   Audience: _____

Writing On Your Own

Suppose you have a friend who may move to your town. You know he likes sports. Write two or three sentences to persuade him to move to your town.

_____

_____

_____

▲ Looking Back

Before you begin to write, decide your purpose for writing (to tell about an event, to describe something, to explain, or to persuade). Also, decide who your audience will be. These two things will help you decide what to write.

From Sentences to Paragraphs

> *In this lesson you will*
> ■ see why people write paragraphs
> ■ get ready to write your own paragraphs

Getting Started

You learned how to write clear, complete sentences in Part A. Good sentences help you tell your ideas to others.

Often you'll want to write more than one sentence about a subject. Your purpose for writing will help determine how much you write.

Say you want to describe yourself. You know many things about yourself. You know how you look, how you feel, what you do, what you think.

When you write about yourself, you want to give quite a few of those details. Then your audience will get a clear picture of you. The details will take more than one or two sentences.

Here are four simple sentences a woman wrote to describe herself.

I am a woman.

I have a family.

I work at a job.

I am happy.

The sentences tell a little about the woman. But to give a clearer picture, she added some details. Her details formed a group of interesting sentences all about one subject — herself:

■ I am a 28-year-old woman. My hair is black, and my eyes are brown. I have a nice family. My husband is 30 years old. He works as a carpenter for a big company.

My children are named Elena and Adam. Elena is seven, and Adam is four. I work as a clerk in a market. I like my job. The people in the market are friendly. I am happy because I have a loving family and a good job.

When you read the sentences, you get a clear picture of the woman. The sentences form a paragraph about the woman. A **paragraph** is a group of sentences written for a certain purpose about the same subject

Here's an Example

Perhaps you want to tell a story about something that happened to you. Even just a short story will take several sentences to tell.

Another purpose is to describe someone or something. You want your reader to know how something looks, smells, tastes, sounds, or feels. You often need more than one sentence for that.

At other times, you want to explain. Maybe you want to write about how to do the laundry or change the oil in a car. You know it can take a while to explain something carefully.

Or your purpose might be to persuade someone. You'll need more than one sentence to get a reader to change his or her mind.

In real life, you usually have to write a number of sentences to tell your message.

Working It Out

Fill in the sentences with words that tell the details about you. The details will describe the kind of person you are.

1. I am a _____ person who is _____
   (what kind)   (how many)
   years old.

2. My eyes are _____ and my hair is _____ .
   (what color)   (what color)

3. I weigh _____ pounds.
   (how many)

4. I like _____ clothes that make me look
   (what kind)
   _____ .
   (how)

"Last night an exciting thing happened to me . . . ."

telling about an event

"Our new house is beautiful . . . ."

describing

"When you do the laundry, make sure you follow these steps . . . ."

explaining

"You should support our clean-up drive for several reasons . . . ."

persuading

5. I _____ when I feel happy.
(do what)

6. When I do not feel happy, I _____ .
(do what)

If you wrote all these sentences in one group, you would have a paragraph describing yourself.

Later in this book, you'll learn how to group your sentences into paragraphs. Good paragraphs make for good writing.

Writing On Your Own

In Getting Started, you read a group of sentences that a woman wrote about herself. In the space below, write a group of sentences that tell about you. You might write about things you like to do, about a funny or sad thing that happened to you, about your family, or about what you do at work, at home, or at school.

▲ Looking Back

You've learned that people write for different purposes. They often need to write a number of detailed sentences to make their writing clear. When a writer writes detailed sentences about one subject, the sentences are a paragraph.

Writing Is a Process

In this lesson you will
- learn the steps in the writing process
- practice the steps by writing a note to a friend

Picture It

In Lesson 2 in Part B, you learned why people write more than one sentence about an idea. You even wrote a few sentences about yourself. These sentences could make a paragraph.

When you cook a meal or build a house, you do it step-by-step. A step-by-step way is called a **process.**

Look at the pictures below. They show the steps in making a house. Each step must be done to make a house that people can live in.

Writing is a process too. It is a step-by-step way to make a note, a letter, a memo, or some other kind of written message.

There are five steps in creating a piece of writing:

1. Think of ideas to write about and list them.   **Prewriting**
2. Write your ideas as sentences.   **Writing**
3. Change, add, or take out words and ideas to make your piece of writing better.   **Revising**

4. Check for mistakes in capitalization, punctuation, spelling, or grammar. **Editing**

5. Write out your final, best copy. **Presenting**

Here's an Example

A woman needs to write a memo about paychecks. The memo is to workers in her office.

First, she thinks of ideas to put in the memo and jots them down. Her list of ideas looks like this. **Prewriting**

paychecks   no more thursday
Friday   after 3 p.m.

The writer looks at these ideas. She decides what her main point is. She plans how she can use the other ideas to explain her main point.

Second, she writes the first draft, or first copy, of her memo. She might write something like this. **Writing**

> **Memo:** This will be the way to pick up paychecks. They will not be picked up on thursday any more Now you will get them on friday. after 3 PM.

Third, the writer changes things to make the writing sound better. She adds words, takes words out, and moves words around. **Revising**

> **Memo:** Their will be a new way to pick up your paychecks Now they can now be picked up on friday after 3 PM, not on thursday

Fourth, the writer looks at her writing. She looks for words spelled wrong, for missing periods, for words that need to start with capital letters, and for other mistakes. She goes through and makes the corrections. **Editing**

MEMO: ~~Their~~ There will be a new way to pick up your paychecks.

Now they can ~~now~~ be picked up on friday F after 3 P.M., not on T thursday.

Fifth, the writer writes out her best copy.   Presenting

> **Memo:** There will be a new way to pick up your paychecks.
> Now they can be picked up on Friday after 3 P.M., not on
> Thursday.

Working It Out

Suppose you want to invite a friend to a birthday party. The
party is for your brother Bob. It will be at your home on Friday,
June 17, at 8 P.M.

First: Jot down ideas you want to include in a note.   **Prewriting**

Second: Write out the invitation in two or three sentences.   **Writing**

Third: Check your invitation. Add anything you need to tell.   **Revising**
Take out any ideas that are not needed. Move ideas around to
sound clear. (Mark your changes in the invitation in step 2.)

Fourth: Read over your invitation. Are all the words spelled   **Editing**
right? Have you written complete sentences? Have you put
periods at the ends of sentences? Have you used capital letters
where you need them? Make any corrections that are needed.

Fifth: Write your best copy of the invitation on a clean piece of   **Presenting**
paper.

➤ Writing On Your Own

Follow the five steps in the writing process to write a note to a
friend. Tell your friend about one of these ideas: your job, your
class, your hobby, your family.

▲ Looking Back

In this lesson you learned that writing is a process with five
steps: prewriting, writing, revising, editing, and presenting.

Getting Ideas: Brainstorming

In this lesson you will

■ find ideas to write about by brainstorming

Getting Started

In the previous lesson, you learned about the steps in the writing process. This lesson will help you with the first step: thinking of ideas to write about.

Have you ever filled out a questionnare in a magazine? You might enjoy filling out the questionnaire on this page.

Read the list of items in the questionnaire. In the blank next to each item, write the letter of the answer that tells what you know about the item.

A = I know a lot about this!
B = I know a little about this.
C = I don't know anything about this.

What Do You Know About . . .

_____ actors	_____ baseball	_____ car engines	_____ gossip
_____ insects	_____ cooking	_____ movies	_____ trucks
_____ dirt bikes	_____ sewing	_____ fishing	_____ racing
_____ horses	_____ jokes	_____ lifesaving	_____ love
_____ horoscopes	_____ puzzles	_____ television	_____ funerals
_____ gardening	_____ pool	_____ card playing	_____ dieting
_____ marriage	_____ rodeos	_____ coffee	_____ prejudice
_____ singing	_____ herbs	_____ housework	_____ teachers
_____ shopping	_____ trivia	_____ music	_____ mountains

Now look at the results. You probably filled in many blanks with an A or a B. What does that mean? It means your mind is full of ideas about many subjects. You may not even realize it.

Sometimes you'll write about things you know a lot about. At other times, as on the GED Test, you may be given a subject to write about. You may think you don't know enough about the subject to write on it. But you probably know more than you think. There is a clever way to find out what you know.

Here's an Example

Suppose someone in a group starts talking about cooking. A man in the group thinks, "I don't know anything about cooking food." He thinks he has nothing to say on the subject. But wait!

The man thinks for a minute. He sometimes grills burgers for his family and friends. Everyone says they taste great.

If the man jotted down all the things he knew about cooking burgers, his list might look like this.

make them nice and flat   put in onion

use garlic salt   a little pepper   watch carefully

my sauce — ketchup, brown sugar, lemon

The list shows the man knew more about cooking than he thought.

Working It Out

Now look at each of the drawings below. Under each drawing, some ideas about the drawing have been written down. Complete the lists with ideas you have about the drawings. One list is done for you.

1. costs less
2. exact change
3. waiting
4. crowded

1. plant in spring
2. tomatoes

1. compare price
2. new or used?

When you filled in your ideas about each picture, you were **brainstorming.** You were looking into your brain to see what you knew. Then you jotted down your ideas in no special order.

Brainstorming is jotting down ideas freely. Brainstorming is a good way to discover ideas to write about.

> **An Idea to Remember**
>
> The process of writing begins when you think of ideas to write about. This step is part of prewriting.

Look back at the words you wrote about one of the pictures. You probably have enough ideas to write a few sentences. For example, from the words under the city bus, you could write these sentences.

The bus costs less than a taxi.
You need exact change, and often it's crowded.
I hate waiting for the bus.

Writing On Your Own

Think about the subject of shopping. In the space below, write down all the ideas that come to your mind about shopping. Don't worry about writing in sentences. Just jot down any ideas that you have.

Now try to use your ideas to write three sentences about shopping.

1. _____

2. _____

3. _____

▲ Looking Back

Brainstorming is jotting down all the ideas that come to mind about a subject. You can find many ideas to write about by brainstorming. Will everyone think of the same ideas? Probably not. Every writer has different ideas on a subject.

Getting Ideas: Asking Questions

In this lesson you will
■ find ideas to write about by asking yourself questions

Picture It

Did you ever see a reporter cover a news story? Did you wonder how the reporter got all the information about the story? The reporter's main job is to get information. Information is gathered by asking questions.

The words that people use to ask questions are **who, what, when, where, why,** and **how.**

Who started the fight?

What exactly happened?

When did the fight start?

Where did the fight take place?

Why were the men fighting?

How badly were the men hurt?

Asking questions is another way to find ideas to write about. When you ask yourself the questions *who, what, when, where, why,* and *how,* your answers will give you ideas to write about.

Here's an Example

Suppose you work in an office. You want to ask people to a party for a worker who is moving away. You decide to write a note to put on the bulletin board. You want to make sure all the information is in the note.

You can write down these questions. They will help you think of all the facts you need. When you answer the questions, your answers will give you ideas to put in the note.

Who?   all people working here are invited

What?   a party for Mel Ward

When?   Friday, January 12, 4 P.M.

Where?   Beck's Cafe on Elm Street

Why?   Mel is moving to Texas

How?   How to respond—tell Rita Finn by
January 8 if you are coming

Working It Out

The following story was in a local newspaper.

John Hays, 25, was injured in a car accident Friday night on Main Street. Hays said the road was icy and he slid into a tree when he tried to turn the corner onto Maple Avenue.

Did the reporter ask questions to get the facts for this story? See if you can answer these questions from the facts in the story.

Who? _____

What happened? _____

When did it happen? _____

Where did it happen? _____

Why did it happen? _____

How did it happen? _____

Prepare to write a letter to a friend. You want to tell about a time you went out and had fun. To get ideas to write about, fill in the facts about this time.

Who went out? _____

What did you do? _____

When did you go? _____

Where did you go? _____

Why was it fun? _____

How did you feel about the event? _____

You might want to use your answers to write a letter to a friend.

Writing On Your Own

Look at the picture below. Ask yourself the questions about what is going on in the picture. Write your answers in the spaces below. Use your imagination!

Who? _____

What? _____

When? _____

Where? _____

Why? _____

How? _____

Now try to use the ideas from your answers to write three sentences about the picture.

1. _____

2. _____

3. _____

▲ Looking Back

You need to think of ideas before you can start to write. Thinking of ideas is part of the prewriting step of the writing process. One way to find ideas is to brainstorm. Another good way is to ask the questions *who, what, when, where, why,* and *how.* Your answers will give you ideas to write about.

Discovering Your Main Idea

> *In this lesson you will*
> - find the main idea of a group of ideas
> - state your main idea

Picture It

Look at the pictures below. Each picture shows a scene in a family's living room.

Which statement tells best what all the pictures show?

A. Everyone feels cozy in the living room.
B. The living room has a TV set and a fireplace.

If you chose the first statement, you were right. That statement sums up the main point of the pictures.

When you write, you have a topic. The **topic** is the subject you plan to write about. If you were going to write about the pictures above, your topic would be "the family living room."

The point you make about your topic is your **main idea.** If you wrote about the pictures above, your main idea would be this: The living room is a cozy place. You would describe each picture. The ideas you write about would tell about that main idea.

The ideas you write down about a topic are like the pictures above. You can discover your own main idea. You do this by thinking about the ideas you've listed.

Here's an Example

Look at the list below. A writer made this list of ideas for a paragraph. His topic was "things to do in winter."

scrape car windows   ski   ice-skate   sit by fire
make snowman with my kids   drink chocolate   shovel snow

Only two of these ideas are work: scraping car windows and shoveling snow. The rest describe fun things to do. So the man's main idea became this: There are many enjoyable things to do in winter.

Maria Nuñez wanted to write about her husband, Juan. Juan was the topic of her paragraph. Here's her list of ideas.

runs a grocery store   tall and slim
thick, wavy hair   big brown eyes   long black eyelashes

Maria looked at her list. Almost all the details help tell about Juan's handsome looks. They give examples of why he's handsome. Maria discovered that her main idea was this: My husband, Juan, is a handsome man.

Working It Out

Look at each of the lists below. Each has five ideas. One idea is a general topic. The other four are details about that topic. Circle the idea that is the **topic** of the list.

A	B	C	D
drink	muscles	hold hands	rent
eat	bones	show love	expenses
dance	nerves	kiss	clothes
party actions	body parts	hug	doctor's bills
talk	blood	give valentines	food

Now, what main idea can you think of that fits the details about each topic? The main idea for list A might be this: People do different things to have fun at a party. For list B, you could say this: The human body is a system of many parts.

Write in a complete sentence a **main idea** for lists C and D.

C. _____

D. _____

Read the following lists of ideas. For each list, decide what could be the main idea of the paragraph. Write the main idea in a sentence on the line below each group.

1. Tom listens to me when I have problems
   helps me when I need it
   likes many things I like
   we have a good time together

Main idea: _____

2. some people like country music
   teenagers like rock
   opera fans
   others like jazz or classical

Main idea: _____

Writing On Your Own

Pick a person who is or was important in your life. The person will be your topic. Your writing will be read by someone who does not know the person. Think about the person for one or two minutes. Write down the ideas that you brainstorm.

Now look at your list of ideas. Do most of the details describe the person? Or do they help explain why the person is important to you? Write a main idea for your paragraph.

▲ Looking Back

Your topic is the subject you want to write about. The main idea is what you want to say about your topic. Discovering your main idea is part of the prewriting step of the writing process.

Selecting Details

> *In this lesson you will*
> - choose details to support a main idea
> - drop details that don't tell about the main idea

Picture It

Pretend you are packing a suitcase to go on a trip to Florida. The pictures below show some things you might pack. Circle the items you would pack.

Did you take the gloves? the furry hat? the boots? the heavy scarf? You probably left them out. You don't need them on a trip to a warm place.

In Lesson 6 in this unit, you learned to discover the main idea of a group of ideas. When you brainstorm, you often come up with a number of different details. Some details will help you write clearly about the main idea. Other details will not. Now you need to choose which details to keep and which ones to leave out.

Here's an Example

Your topic is making a pizza. You write down this list of details:

roll out dough   pizza makes you thirsty
put crust in pizza pie pan   mix shortening with flour
add ⅓ cup water   put cheese and toppings on
Jan likes everything on hers   spread tomato sauce on crust
bake in oven 1 hour at 350°

After looking at those ideas, you decide on your main idea:
Making a pizza takes several careful steps. Then you look again
at your list. All the details are needed to tell about this main
idea except these two:
1. pizza makes you thirsty
2. Jan likes everything on hers
You want to leave out these details when you write. They don't
really tell about making a pizza.

Working It Out

In each list, there is a main idea. There are also some details
that might be used to tell about the main idea. Draw a line
through any idea that does *not* tell about the main idea.

1. **Main Idea:** A person can choose from many careers.
   Details:
   nurse   clerk   pay
   plumber   vacation   janitor

2. **Main Idea:** I enjoy working outdoors.
   Details:
   fresh air   heat of sun   Dad is an office worker
   sounds of birds   pays less than office job   bright light of sun

3. **Main Idea:** Watching TV can be good.
   Details:
   reading is better   kids learn ABCs   relaxing after work
   learn the news   boring   family can do it together

4. Read the following paragraph. Cross out the sentences that do *not* tell about the main idea. These sentences don't belong in the paragraph.

Street people are people who need help. They eat food from garbage cans. They sleep in the street. The streets are lined with stores. In winter, they have no place to go to get warm. People who are sick need help too. Someone should do something for these people.

⟹ *Writing On Your Own*

Most people try to stay healthy. Use the topic "How I Keep Healthy." In the space below, list all the details that come to mind when you think about this topic. Next, write a statement of your main idea. Then go back and choose *only* those details that tell about how you keep healthy. Cross out all the other details.

▲ Looking Back

When you write about a main idea, use only the details that tell about that main idea. Leave out all other ideas. Choosing your details is part of the prewriting step of the writing process.

Outlining Your Ideas

In this lesson you will

■ organize your ideas by making an outline, or plan

Picture It

Many people have calendars like this one. They write things they plan to do in the boxes. The calendar helps them organize their days. They know just what day they will do certain things.

In the previous lesson, you learned to choose details to support your main idea. Now you need to organize your ideas. You need to make a plan like the plans on the calendar. Your plan will help you see where to put each idea. This plan is called an **outline.** An outline is set up like this.

You write down the main idea first.

1. Under it, you list the details you will use to tell about the main idea.

   Under each detail, you list ideas about the detail that you want to put in your piece of writing.

Here's an Example

Say you need to write directions for someone. You need to explain how to clean an office.

To give the cleaner a plan for the job, you write an outline that looks like this.

How to Clean the Office

1. Get the cleaning tools

2. Clean the office

3. Put away the tools

This outline is a good start for the plan. But it doesn't give the person enough information. You need to tell more about the three topics — getting the tools, cleaning, and putting away the tools.

So you add some more ideas to your outline. Your new outline looks like this:

How to Clean the Office

1. Get the cleaning tools
     tools in Room 235
     vacuum cleaner
     mop and pail
     soap and water

2. Clean the office
     mop the floor
     vacuum the carpet

3. Put away tools
     dump soapy water in drain in hall
     put tools in Room 235

Now you have a clear plan for cleaning the office.

Working It Out

Julia wanted to make a poster about her garage sale. First she made a list of all her ideas for the poster. Then she started to make an outline to organize her ideas. Look at the rest of her list on the left. Help her complete her outline. Write the words from the list in their proper places in the boxed outline.

Sunday, June 11
bikes
green house with black
    shutters
clothing
rain dates—June 17 and 18
Place

```
┌─────────────────────────────┐
│ Garage Sale                 │
│ Time                        │
│    Saturday, June 10        │
│    _____      │
│                             │
│    9–5 each day             │
│    _____      │
│                             │
│    _____      │
│    102 Third Street         │
│    follow signs on          │
│       Grant Avenue          │
│    _____      │
│                             │
│ Things for Sale             │
│    _____      │
│                             │
│    furniture                │
│    books                    │
│    _____      │
└─────────────────────────────┘
```

Writing On Your Own

Pretend you want to write a letter to a friend. You want to
explain what you do during a normal week. In one part, tell
what you do on weekdays. In a second part, list what you do on
weekends. Brainstorm for ideas. Then make an outline of those
ideas.

▲ Looking Back

In this lesson you learned that you need to make a plan when
you write. The plan helps you organize your ideas. This plan is
an **outline.** The outline puts the main idea as a heading. It lists
the details under the heading. Making an outline is part of the
prewriting step of the writing process.

Mapping Your Ideas

In this lesson you will

■ organize your ideas by mapping

Picture It

In the previous lesson, you learned that part of prewriting is organizing your ideas. One way to do this is to outline them. Another way to organize ideas is to map them. A **map** is a picture of the main ideas and details to use in writing.

Do you remember learning about the United States when you were young? You probably used a map to help you. The map made it easier for you to see the states. You could see how big each state was. You could see where each state was located. The map helped you organize some ideas about the country.

A map helps you organize your writing ideas too. The picture can help you *see* a main idea. It can help you see the details that tell about the main idea.

Here's an Example

Carlos and Maria Mendoza are going to the grocery store. They want to make a plan. The plan will help them do their shopping quickly. They make a map so that each will know what to buy. Their map looks like this:

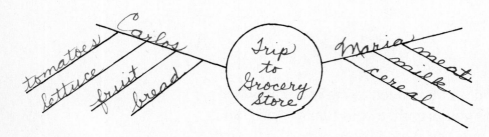

Here's another example. John Oates is in charge of a crew. Frank, Luther, and Mike are on the crew. They are making an empty lot into a park.

John wants to plan the job. He makes a map to help him organize his ideas.

To make a map, John draws a circle in the middle of a sheet of paper. He writes his main idea in the circle. Then he writes the most important ideas about the main idea. They are written on branches that come out from the circle. Last, he adds details about each of the important ideas. They are written on branches that come out from the main branches.

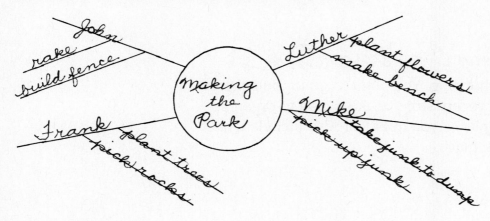

Working It Out

In a family, every person has jobs around the house. A family started this map to organize their jobs. Fill in the blank parts of the map. Be sure every member has some jobs to do around the house.

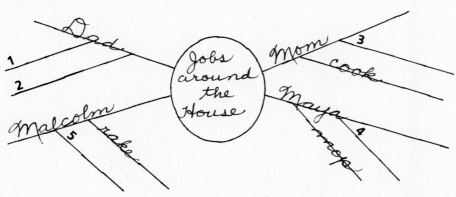

A writer is planning a letter to a friend from Italy. His friend will be visiting New York for a whole year. The writer wants to tell the friend what clothes to bring for each season. He makes a map to organize his ideas. Fill in the blank parts of his map.

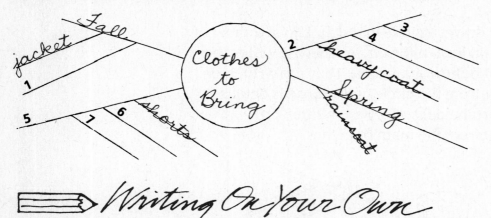

✏️ Writing On Your Own

Suppose you're going shopping. You want to go to the bakery, the drugstore, and the grocery store. Make a map to organize your ideas. Include the places you must go. Also include what you want to buy at each place.

▲ Looking Back

Before you write, you need to organize your ideas. You can use an outline, or you can use a map. A map gives you a picture of the way you will organize your main idea and details. Making a map is part of the prewriting step of the writing process.

Writing the First Draft

Your Topic Sentence

In this lesson you will
■ write a topic sentence

Picture It

Suppose you see this list on a poster at work. You wonder, "What is this all about?"

Keep warm.	**Drink plenty of liquids.**
Take aspirin.	**Get lots of rest.**

Then a woman writes this at the top: *These are ways to get over a cold or the flu.* She has put the main idea in a sentence. Now you understand the message.

In Lesson 6 in Part B, you learned that you need a main idea when you write. This idea tells what you are writing about. You need to write this main idea in a sentence. This helps your reader understand your message.

The **topic sentence** is the sentence that states your main idea. It states in a complete sentence what you are writing about. Writing the topic sentence is the beginning of the second step in the whole writing process. You have done your prewriting. Now you're ready to start writing. You'll write the **first draft,** or copy, of your paragraph.

An Idea to Remember

Write a topic sentence in good sentence form. Give it a subject and a verb. Be sure it tells a complete thought.

Here's an Example

A cook wrote this paragraph about soup.

■ Soup is an easy meal to make. First, you boil water in a big pan. Next, you cut up meat and vegetables into small pieces. Then you put the meat and vegetables into the boiling water. Finally, you let it all cook for two to three hours. Then you have a nice meal to put on the table.

The main idea of this paragraph is how easy it is to make soup. The writer put this idea in a complete sentence. The topic sentence is the first sentence in the paragraph. The next four sentences tell about the topic sentence. They tell the easy steps in making soup. The last sentence sums up the message.

Here's another example. This paragraph is about walking.

■ Walking gives your body exercise. Your heart and leg muscles get a real workout. It makes you get out in the fresh air. Breathing good air is healthy for your lungs. It also gives you a chance to relax and think. Walking is good for you.

The main idea of this paragraph is that walking is good for you. The writer put this idea in a topic sentence. The topic sentence is the *last* sentence this time. All the other sentences tell why walking is good.

The topic sentence usually goes at the beginning of your piece of writing. Sometimes you may want to put it at the end.

Working It Out

A. Read each group of words below. Decide if it could be a topic sentence for a paragraph. Put a check next to it if it could. Remember: A topic sentence tells a main idea and is written as a complete sentence.

_____ The best day I ever had.
_____ Sherman is a clever basketball player.
_____ Rainy days.
_____ How to make french fries.
_____ My company is made up of three parts.
_____ Finding a husband is a hard task.

B. Now read each piece of writing that follows. Choose a good topic sentence from the ones listed. Write it on the blank line.

1. Checkers has been a favorite game for many years. Cards is another game that many people enjoy. My family has always liked to play Monopoly and Parcheesi.
   A. My favorite game is Monopoly.
   B. People all over the world play cards.
   C. Games are a popular way to spend free time.

Topic sentence: _____

2. The party will be at Rosa Joy's house. It will be on Saturday at 8 P.M. You can bring a birthday gift for Rosa if you want.
   A. Go out and buy a present for Rosa.
   B. There is going to be a birthday party.
   C. I like parties of all kinds.

Topic sentence: _____

➤ Writing On Your Own

Read the following paragraph. On the line write a topic sentence that states the main idea of the paragraph.

_____

I like the talk shows. The host talks with famous people every day. My husband enjoys the news programs. Every night from six to seven, he sits and watches them to learn about the world. The kids, of course, like the cartoons and "Sesame Street." These shows make them laugh and teach them things.

   Now write a paragraph of at least four or five sentences on your own paper. Tell about a TV show you like. First, do your prewriting. Next, write a topic sentence that states the main idea of the paragraph. Then write sentences that tell about the topic sentence.

▲ Looking Back

The topic sentence tells the main idea of a piece of writing. It is a complete sentence. A topic sentence is part of the second step of the writing process — writing a first draft.

Supporting Details

> *In this lesson you will*
> ■ write sentences giving details to support your main idea

Picture It

I get washed.

I brush my teeth.

I get dressed.

I cook breakfast.

I eat.

These drawings show **details.** You could use these details in a paragraph. The main idea of the paragraph would be getting ready for work. The topic sentence for the paragraph could be this: *Each morning I do several things to get ready for work.* The details all tell about that main idea.

In Lesson 7 in Part B, you chose details to support a main idea. Now you'll see how to write details in a paragraph. You need to write the details in complete sentences. Each will tell about the main idea stated in your topic sentence. That's why these sentences are called **supporting details.**

An Idea to Remember

When you write details in sentences, you're writing a first draft. In your first draft, don't worry about mistakes! Just get all your ideas down on paper. That's what a first draft is for. You'll get a chance to change and fix things later.

Here's an Example

Say you plan to write a note about a neighborhood meeting. You make the following list of ideas.

Tuesday, May 12, 7 P.M.   volunteers

Baker School   help with street fair

Room 210   May 25–26, 10 A.M. to 8 P.M.

You decide on your main idea. It is that there's going to be a meeting. You write it in this topic sentence: *There will be an important meeting.*

Now you need to put your supporting details into sentences too. All these sentences need to tell about the meeting. Your note might end up looking like this.

> There will be an important meeting. It will be on Tuesday, May 12, at 7 P.M. It will be in Room 210 at Baker School. This meeting is for volunteers who can help with the street fair on May 25–26 from 10 A.M. to 8 P.M.

Working It Out

A. You want to write about movies. Your topic sentence is this: *There are many different kinds of movies for people to see.* List four details you could use to support this main idea. Then write each as a sentence.

1. _____

_____

2. _____

_____

3. _____

_____

4. _____

_____

B. Here's a set of ideas from one writer. The ideas are for a paragraph about traffic lights.

tell drivers what to do
red — on top — Stop
yellow — middle — light is changing — careful
green — on bottom — Go

The writer decided on this topic sentence: *Traffic lights give important directions.* Use the details listed to write four or five sentences that support this main idea. The last sentence sums up the paragraph.

Traffic lights give important directions. _____

_____

_____

_____

_____

_____ Traffic lights prevent many accidents.

✏️ *Writing On Your Own*

Take this topic sentence: *There are many means of transportation that people can use today.* List four details you can use to tell about this main idea.

1. _____

2. _____

3. _____

4. _____

First, prewrite on your own paper. Make a map or an outline. Then write your topic sentence. After that, write at least four more sentences. In each sentence, tell about one of the details you listed. Then sum up the paragraph in the last sentence.

▲ Looking Back

The topic sentence in a paragraph tells the main idea. The next sentences give details that support the main idea. Often the last sentence sums up the paragraph. Writing these sentences is part of the second step in the writing process—writing a first draft.

Developing Details

> *In this lesson you will*
> ■ explain your supporting details

Picture It

Look at each picture. You get a much clearer idea of things in the second picture. The artist has "filled in" all the details.

In the previous lesson, you wrote sentences about details. The details support the main idea of a paragraph. They give your reader a clearer idea of your message. But you need to do more than just state your details. You also need to "fill in," or explain them a little.

Facts, examples, and reasons are some ways you can explain your ideas.

■ *Facts* are specific numbers, names, places, things, and events. They inform your reader about your ideas.

■ *Examples* are specific people, places, things, and events. They are real-life instances of ideas.

■ *Reasons* are ideas that show why something happens or is true.

Here's an Example

Say your boss makes this rule: People who want a raise have to explain why they should get one. You make this list.

I deserve a raise.

1. I work hard.
2. I work overtime.
3. I am responsible.

You have three good reasons. But your reasons are very general. The boss might say, "Prove that you work hard." You need to give specific examples to explain your reasons. You might list examples like this.

I deserve a raise.

1. I work hard
   I wrap 100 packages each day.
   I sort and deliver all mail each day.
   I keep the mail room neat and clean.
2. I work overtime.
   I worked until 7 P.M. every day last month to complete rush orders.
3. I am responsible.
   I always punch in on time.
   I complete all my jobs on time.

Now the boss should give you the raise!

Working It Out

Ann is writing a letter to Glenn. Glenn is thinking of coming to Ann's city for a vacation. Ann wants to persuade him to come. She tells Glenn it will be fun and interesting.

■ Come to Boston for your vacation! There are many things you can do for fun. You can lie on the beach or swim. You can see a baseball game. The ball park is near my home. There are also many interesting places to visit. One day you can go to the Old State House and the Old North Church. They are important spots in our country's history. You can also visit the site of the Battle of Bunker Hill. Come here on vacation! We'll have a great time!

What specific examples does Ann give?

Examples of things that are fun to do:

1. _____

2. _____

Examples of interesting places to go:

3. _____

4. _____

Writing On Your Own

A woman wants to write a letter. Her main idea is to persuade her friend to stop smoking. She has listed two details to persuade her friend to quit. She needs to explain those details to make them clearer and stronger. Under each detail, put two reasons she could use.

Detail: **You will feel better.**

1. _____

2. _____

Detail: **You will look better.**

3. _____

4. _____

Now write a paragraph of at least six or seven sentences on your own paper. Persuade the friend to quit smoking. Use the reasons and details from above.

▲ Looking Back

Details support your main idea. But you need to do more than just state the details. You need to explain them. You can explain them by using facts, examples, and reasons when you write your first draft.

Relating Ideas:
Time Order and Cause/Effect

In this lesson you will
- see how details may be related in time
- see how details may be causes and effects

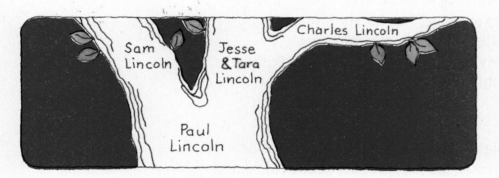

Picture It

This is a family tree. It shows how people in a family are related to each other. For example, Jesse Lincoln is—

1. Paul Lincoln's son
2. Charles Lincoln's father
3. Tara Lincoln's husband
4. Sam Lincoln's brother

Jesse is related to the people in his family in many ways.

You've been writing supporting details in paragraphs. Often those details are related in certain ways too.

Time is one way that details may be related. First, one thing happens; second, another thing happens; and so on.

Sometimes one thing doesn't just happen before another. The first event actually *causes* the second to happen. This **cause-and-effect** connection is another way details may be related. A cause makes something happen. The effect is the thing made to happen.

Here's an Example

A man was good at giving parties. He wrote this paragraph to explain how to do it. His details are in time order.

- Planning a party is easy. First, you invite the people you want to come. Second, you buy the food and drinks. The day of the party, you clean your house. Then you put out the food and drinks on a table. Put on some good music too. Finally, you welcome your guests to the party.

The writer told about the actions in the time order in which they happen. This order makes his ideas clear to you.

Another person wrote this paragraph. She was reviewing a restaurant. Her details are causes and their effects.

- The Park Cafe serves excellent food. As a result, they do a very good business. People stand in line waiting to get into the cafe. So the manager has had to hire more workers. Some of these waiters lack experience. Because of that, service is not as good. Let's hope the cafe solves this problem soon.

Working It Out

A. A man wants to explain how to give a dog a bath. He lists the following details to use in his paragraph. Number the details in the order in which he should put them.

_____ Rinse the soap off the dog.

_____ Rub the dog with a towel.

_____ Put soap on the wet dog.

_____ Get water, soap, and towels.

_____ Scrub the dog.

_____ Wet the dog all over.

B. A woman is writing a letter. She wants to explain why she had a bad day. She has listed reasons below. Number her details to show which causes led to which effects.

_____ Since I got home so late, I missed my favorite TV show.

_____ My alarm clock didn't go off, so I was late for work.

_____ Then the computers went down. Because I had to do everything by hand, I had to work very late.

_____ As a result, my boss was angry at me.

C. Each sentence below describes a cause. Write a sentence that states what could be an effect. The first pair is done to help you get started.

1. *Cause:* Pete loved his new car.

   Effect: He washed and waxed it all the time.

2. *Cause:* Lisa had not heard from Jim in a week.

   Effect: _____

3. *Cause:* You feel very sick.

   Effect: _____

4. *Cause:* You study hard for a test.

   Effect: _____

Writing On Your Own

A. Write a paragraph of at least four or five sentences. Tell how to plan to write a paragraph. Put your topic sentence first. Then put your other sentences in time order. Don't forget to prewrite!

_____

_____

_____

_____

B. Write a paragraph of at least four or five sentences. Tell about the different kinds of weather and the effects they have on you. Don't forget to prewrite.

_____

_____

_____

_____

▲ Looking Back

When you write, your details are related in some way. The details may be related in time. They may also be causes and effects.

Relating Ideas:
Order of Importance and Comparison/Contrast

> *In this lesson you will*
> ■ see how details can be listed in order of importance
> ■ see how details may compare or contrast things

Picture It

You've just learned how details may be related. Details may follow a time order. They may be causes and effects. You may also find your details for a paragraph are related in other ways.

Details may differ in their importance. Writers will put such details in **order of importance.** News stories are written this way. The most important details come first. The least important details come last. The example at the right helps you picture this order in a story.

A boy was saved from drowning today by two brave men. Joshua Hill, age 4, was swimming at Long Beach with his family. He started to go under the waves. Manuel Nuñez, 20, and Luis Perillo, 19, pulled Joshua to shore. The doctors say the boy will be fine.

Now look at these pictures. What would you write about the homes in the pictures? You might **compare** them to show how they are alike. Or you might **contrast** them to show how they are different. Your details will be related. They will tell about likenesses, differences, or both.

You can choose the order of your details when you list them. You can also choose their order when you compare or contrast things.

Here's an Example

A clerk wrote this paragraph about her budget. She put the most important ideas first. She wrote the least important ones last.

■ I am very careful about spending my money. When I get paid, I pay my bills. These bills are for rent, heat, and food. Some of the money left is put in my savings. Any extra money is used to buy new clothes or to go out for a good time.

A salesman wrote this next paragraph. He wanted to show how traveling is different from being at home. He contrasted the two point by point.

■ Being away from home is very different from being in my own house. At home, I have my own bed and all my familiar belongings. When I am away, I have to sleep in a strange bed. Also, all the things around me belong to a hotel. At home, I cook the foods I like best. Away from home, I have to eat what is served in restaurants. I like life at home better than life away from home.

Working It Out

A. A writer wants to put the following details in a paragraph. He wants to write them in order from *least* important to *most* important. Number the sentences in the order he should write them. The topic sentence has been numbered 1 to get you started.

___1___ People should eat healthy foods.

_____ They will look slim and trim.

_____ They will live longer.

_____ They will probably save money on groceries.

_____ They will feel better.

B. Another writer wants to write about city life and country life. She wants to show the differences between the two. Below are the details for her paragraph. Number the details in the order *you* would put them. The topic sentence has been numbered 1 to get you started.

_____ The country is quiet and calm.

_____ The city is crowded.

__1__ City life and country life are very different.

_____ The city is noisy and busy.

_____ Most city people work in offices and big stores.

_____ The country has lots of room to move around.

_____ Many country people work on farms or in small stores.

Writing On Your Own

A. Write a paragraph of at least four or five sentences. Tell why you think people should be able to read. Put your ideas in order of importance from *most* important to *least* important. Don't forget to prewrite.

_____

_____

_____

_____

B. Write a paragraph of at least four or five sentences contrasting two homes. Tell the differences in size, color, and location. Prewrite before you write.

_____

_____

_____

_____

▲ Looking Back

Sometimes you can list your details in order of their importance. Sometimes your details will show points of comparison or contrast. These are two other ways of relating details when you write your first draft.

Improving
What You Write

Revising Your Work

> *In this lesson you will*
> ■ improve your first draft

Picture It

You've learned to write the first draft of a paragraph. Now you're ready for the next step in the writing process.

Dipak Gupta was in charge of a poster for a town celebration. A printer would make many copies of the poster. They would be put all over the town for people to read.

Dipak read the poster carefully. He wanted to make sure it was right before copies were made. He asked himself:

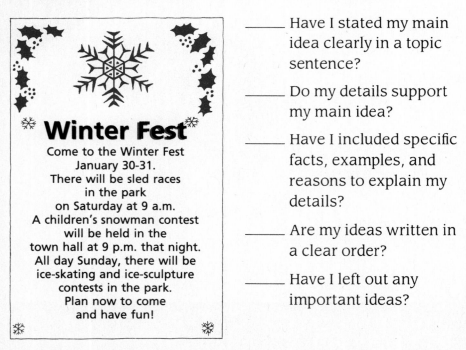

Winter Fest
Come to the Winter Fest
January 30-31.
There will be sled races
in the park
on Saturday at 9 a.m.
A children's snowman contest
will be held in the
town hall at 9 p.m. that night.
All day Sunday, there will be
ice-skating and ice-sculpture
contests in the park.
Plan now to come
and have fun!

_____ Have I stated my main idea clearly in a topic sentence?

_____ Do my details support my main idea?

_____ Have I included specific facts, examples, and reasons to explain my details?

_____ Are my ideas written in a clear order?

_____ Have I left out any important ideas?

Dipak tried to improve the poster by asking these questions. You also need to read your first draft several times. You'll be able to change and improve it. The best writers *always* change and improve their first draft.

Changing and improving a first draft is called **revising.** When you revise, you make your writing as clear as possible. To help you revise, you can ask the questions Dipak did.

Here's an Example

A woman wrote this first draft to explain some effects of dieting.

- Dieting can help you lose weight. It also helps you look better. You begin to look slim instead of chubby. It can help you feel good about the way you look. But dieting can also make you eat wrong. You might eat nothing, or you might eat foods that are not really healthy. For example, you might eat cake and then nothing else all day. Then you might even get sick from dieting.

The woman read what she had written several times. She asked herself these questions:

- Have I stated my main idea clearly in a topic sentence?
  No. I should write a good topic sentence. I'll add this at the beginning: *Dieting can have good and bad results.*
- Do my details support my main idea?
  Yes. The good results are that you lose weight, you look better, and you feel good. The bad results are that you may eat wrong and you may get sick.
- Have I included specific facts, examples, and reasons to explain my details?
  Yes. You look slim instead of chubby, and you may eat cake and nothing else.
- Are my ideas written in a clear order?
  Yes. I talked first about the good effects of dieting. Then I talked about the bad effects.
- Have I left out any important ideas?
  I could explain the detail about feeling good. I'll add this after the fourth sentence: *When you feel attractive, your self-image is good.*

The writer went back to her paragraph to revise it. She did not copy it over. She just wrote her changes on the first draft.

Working It Out

Read this "letter to the editor." Use the questions after the paragraph to help you revise it.

■ Two dead trees on State Street should be cut down. They don't look very nice. They might fall and kill or hurt someone. People walk along or drive down the street all the time. During a storm, they might be blown down on a nearby house. There are two houses near each tree. These trees need to be cut down.

1. Is there a sentence that states the main idea? If so, what is it?

_____

2. What details are used to support the main idea? Do they support it?

_____

3. Is there an example, fact, or reason to explain each detail? If not, what could you add?

_____

4. Could the details be put in a better order? If so, how?

_____

Writing On Your Own

Write a paragraph of at least four or five sentences. Your topic is the differences between you and another member of your family. Prewrite before you write your first draft. Use your own paper.

Now revise your paragraph. Ask yourself the questions on page 156 about your first draft.

▲ Looking Back

After you write your first draft, you need to revise it. Check it for these things: the main idea (topic sentence), specific supporting details, order of ideas, and other possible ideas to put in. Improve it any way you can.

Tying It All Together

> **In this lesson you will**
> - link sentences in paragraphs

Picture It

Nails are important!

When people build a house, they make a plan first. Then they get together all their materials. At this point, all they have is a heap of boards, windows, and doors. They have to connect all those materials. Then the house will take shape.

Nails are important because they connect the materials to make a house.

When you write, it is a little like building a house. You make a plan. You learned how to do that in Lessons 4–9 in Part B of this book. Then you write your ideas in sentences. You learned how to write such a first draft in Lessons 10–14. These sentences need to be connected too. When they are connected, your whole paragraph will take shape. Then it will make sense to your reader.

You can use certain words to tie together sentences. If you forget them in your first draft, you can put them in when you revise.

Here's an Example

Suppose your sentences tell ideas in **time** order. You can use linking words like the following:

first	First, you get a snack in the kitchen.
second	Second, you take your snack to the living room.
then	Then, you turn on the TV.
next	Next, you sit in a soft chair.
finally	Finally, you relax after a hard day's work.

Suppose your sentences deal with **causes and effects.** You can use linking words like these:

because	Because he was clumsy, he fell down the stairs.
as a result	As a result of the fall, he broke his leg.

Other linking words for causes and effects are these: *for that reason, since, so, consequently,* and *therefore.*

When you tell ideas in **order of importance,** you can use linking words like these:

first	First, I would spend time with my children.
next	Next, I would do housework.

You can link sentences that **compare** ideas by using these words:

also	Kenji has black hair also.
likewise	Likewise, Jolita speaks Spanish.

Other linking words for comparison are *similarly* and *too.*

You can link sentences that **contrast** ideas by using these words:

although	Although Marcia is tall, her sister is not.
in contrast	In contrast, her sister is very sweet.

Other linking words for contrast are *but, however, nevertheless, on the other hand, while,* and *yet.*

When you give an **example,** you can use a linking word like this:

for example	For example, yellow is a cheery color.

For instance and *such as* can also give examples.

When you are **ending** your paragraph, you can use a linking word like this:

finally	Finally, the game was over.

In conclusion, then, and *last* also show you are ending your paragraph.

Working It Out

A. Use linking words from Here's an Example to fill in the blanks below. Use a word that makes the meaning of each pair of sentences clear.

1. First, turn the key. _____ step on the gas pedal.

2. Julio felt sick. _____ he went to the doctor.

3. Joe was scared. _____ Ben was calm.

4. Carl lives in Chicago. _____ Ann lives in a big city.

5. I like collecting things. _____ I have many stamps and more than 100 old bottles.

B. Now read the first draft of a paragraph below. Help the writer revise it. Fill in linking words in the blanks. Choose from the ones in Here's an Example. Be sure they tie the sentences together.

My wedding day was a tense day! _____ , I woke up late and had to skip breakfast. _____ , I tore a hole in my tux. _____ my car broke down, and so did the car of my best man! When we _____ got to the church, I found that I had left the rings at home. _____ , my wedding day could have gone a lot more smoothly.

Writing On Your Own

Write a paragraph of five or six sentences on your own paper. Tell the effects a cold or the flu has on you. Use four of the following linking words to connect your sentences. Prewrite, write your first draft, and then revise.

| because | as a result | for that reason | consequently |
| since | therefore | for example | such as |

▲ Looking Back

When you write, you need to connect your ideas. Then the whole paragraph will be clear to your reader. You can use certain words to link the ideas in sentences. When you revise, ask yourself, "Did I connect my ideas with linking words?"

Varying Your Sentences

In this lesson you will
- write different types of sentences

Picture It

People like variety! They get bored if they have to eat the same food every day. They find life dull if they have to do the same things every day.

When you write, you need some variety too. Sentences are more interesting to read if they don't all sound the same.

You can vary your sentences when you write and revise. Here are some ways to add variety to your sentences.

- Mix long and short sentences.
- Use statements, questions, exclamations, and commands.
- Change the beginnings of sentences.

Here's an Example

Mixing long and short sentences—
This writer used too many short, simple sentences. His paragraph sounds choppy and simple.

- The waitress is young. She works at the Fifth Avenue Diner. She is 21. Her name is Lisa. She is pretty. Lisa smiles and talks to everyone. She is always friendly. Everyone likes her.

The man's paragraph sounded better once he revised. He used long and short sentences. Then his paragraph sounded like this.

■ Lisa is a 21-year-old waitress at the Fifth Avenue Diner. She is pretty. Because she is friendly, Lisa smiles and talks to everyone. Everyone likes her.

Using statements, questions, exclamations, and commands—
Many writers use statements for all their sentences. Sometimes it is interesting to use a question, an exclamation, or a command for variety. This woman used a question.

■ Why do I want to be a nurse? First, I like to help people. Sick people need my help. That makes me feel good. Second, I like medical work. I think it's interesting. Nursing will be a good career for me.

Using different beginnings for sentences—
In this paragraph, all the sentences start the same way.

■ We had our wedding in a big church. We had many people there. We had a party afterward. We had the party in a nice hall. We had a band play music. We danced and sang at the party. We had a nice wedding day.

The writer revised his paragraph. This time he didn't start every sentence with "We." He used different beginnings.

■ Our wedding was held in a big church. Happily, we had many people there. After the wedding, we had a party in a nice hall. A band played music. Because we were so happy, we sang and danced at the party. We had a nice wedding day.

Working It Out

A. Combine the sentences in each pair below. Then you will have revised two short, choppy sentences into one longer sentence.

1. Jim ate too much pizza. He became very sick.

_____

2. She focused her camera. She took our picture.

_____

B. Suppose you're writing about dogs. Below, write three sentences about dogs. Make sure each is the kind of sentence that is named.

1. a question: _____

2. a command: _____

3. an exclamation: _____

C. Suppose you want to revise these sentences. You want to start them in different ways. Make the underlined part the beginning of each sentence.

1. Joe was tired <u>by the time the game began</u>.

_____

2. Mr. Kane repeated the words <u>slowly</u>.

_____

✏️➡ *Writing On Your Own*

Prewrite about a game you enjoy playing or watching. Then write a first draft of a paragraph on that topic below. Write five or six sentences. Include long and short sentences. Write a question, an exclamation, or a command. Start your sentences in different ways. When you revise, see if you can vary your sentences more.

_____

_____

_____

_____

_____

▲ Looking Back

When you write, use a variety of sentences. Your writing will sound more interesting. Three ways you can vary your sentences are by using (1) both long and short sentences, (2) questions, exclamations, and commands, and (3) different kinds of beginnings. When you revise, ask yourself, ''Did I use a variety of sentences?''

Choosing the Best Words

> *In this lesson you will*
> ■ use specific words
> ■ use concise wording

Picture It

You know it's important to write your ideas clearly. When you revise, you can make sure you've done just that.

One way to improve your writing is to use **specific** words. *Specific* words are precise words. Suppose a friend told you she had bought an animal. What picture would come to mind?

The word *animal* is too general. You don't know what animal to picture. If your friend had said "cat," the idea would have been clearer.

When you write and revise, use specific words. Then your reader will have a clear picture of your ideas.

Another way to improve your writing is to use **concise** wording. *Concise* means "as few words as possible." Suppose you receive this note. What do you think it says?

> The thing is that no one knows the answer on account of the fact that the letter that we received was written down in a not very clear way.

The note is confusing. The writer used many extra words that he didn't need. He could have simply written this.

> No one knows the answer because the letter we received was not clear.

When you write and revise, use just the words you really need. Concise writing is clearer and more interesting. It comes right to the point.

Be specific (precise) and short (concise) when you write and revise.

Here's an Example

Read the following sentences about a man and a child.

- A man walked across the yard. He saw a child standing on the porch of the house and spoke to the child.

What did you picture in your mind? Did you see a young man strolling to a ranch house and joking with a toddler? Or an old gentleman hobbling toward a mansion and whispering to a baby? Or an angry man stamping toward a shack and yelling at a boy?

The writer should have revised her writing to use specific words. They would give you a clearer picture of her message.

General word	Specific words
man	young man, old gentleman, angry man
walked	strolled, hobbled, stamped
child	toddler, baby, boy
house	ranch house, mansion, shack
spoke	joked, whispered, yelled

The following memo is not concise. It uses too many words.

> Memo: These days all people who work in the office here should be on time for the job that they have here.

The writer revised the memo this way.

> Memo: All office workers should be on time for work.

Working It Out

A. For each word below, list three specific words. They should mean almost the same thing as the general word.

1. storm   _____   _____   _____

2. cook   _____   _____   _____

3. eat   _____   _____   _____

B. Revise each sentence below. Leave out the underlined words. They are not needed.

1. The huge fish weighed more than 100 pounds <u>in weight</u>.

2. The party began at 8 P.M. <u>at night</u>.

 *Writing On Your Own*

A. Read this first draft. Revise the paragraph on your own paper. Put in a specific word or phrase for each **bold** word.

■ We like to have parties **there**. It is a **nice** place. Everyone has a **great** time. We **drink** lots of soda and **eat** huge amounts of good **food**. People play **games** and listen to **good** music. It is always fun.

B. Now read this wordy paragraph. Revise the paragraph on your own paper. Leave out any words that are not needed. You can also change the wording if you want. Improve the paragraph any way you can.

■ What I want to say is that people who have a pair of two twins have a job that is hard to do. This is true because of the fact that there is twice the work. The people who are the parents of baby twins are just beginning years of taking care of two children who are alike and similar.

▲ Looking Back

Use specific words to give your reader a clear picture of your ideas. Also, be concise. Use only the words you really need. When you revise, ask yourself, "Did I use specific, concise words?"

Editing Guidelines

> **In this lesson you will**
> ■ work with guidelines for editing your writing

Picture It

This man is going to apply for a job. He wants to look good. He carefully chose his suit and dressed. Yet he still doesn't look quite right. He needs to fix the small matters.

When you write, you want to "look good." You want to create writing that is clear and easy to read. Prewriting, writing a first draft, and revising help you do that. But before you're through, you also need to **edit,** or fix the small matters. You need to check your—

- capitalization
- spelling
- punctuation
- grammar

Here's an Example

Here is a guide you can use when you edit your writing.

Editing Guide

Capitalization

1. Capitalize the first word in a sentence.

2. Capitalize the names of specific people, places, and things.
John Zack   the United States   Ford Motor Company

3. Capitalize the first word and all other important words in a title.
The New York Times   Gone with the Wind

4. Capitalize the word *I.*

5. Capitalize the names of events in history and special events.
Civil War   Olympics

---

6. Capitalize names on the calendar.
Monday   September   Fourth of July

7. Capitalize the names of nationalities and religions.
Italian   Catholic

8. Capitalize the brand names of products.
Buick   Kleenex   Coca-Cola

9. Capitalize titles used in front of people's names.
Mr. Finn   Senator Valdez   Doctor Koehl

Punctuation

Period

1. Use a period at the end of a statement or command.
I arrived at midnight.   Bring me the TV guide.

2. Use periods after abbreviations and initials.
Mrs.   Co.   Jr.   A.M.   S. M. Brown

Comma

1. Use a comma after each item in a series.
eggs, bread, milk, and cheese

2. Use a comma to separate words that describe a noun *if* you could also just say "and" between them.
the two big, ugly dogs   (the two big and ugly dogs)

3. Use a comma when you need to make a brief pause in reading a sentence.
Stefan, on the other hand, is big and strong.
When we saw the storm coming, we ran for cover.

4. Use a comma between city and state and also day and year.
Albany, New York   June 17, 1982

Spelling

■ Take time to read, hear, and say words correctly.
■ Learn to sound out a word by its parts.
sep-a-rate   ar-ti-cle   to-geth-er   un-der-neath
■ List words you spell wrong, and study them. Find each one in a dictionary, write it, and spell it aloud. These rules can help you spell words many people have trouble with.

1. When the letters *i* and *e* rhyme with "me," write *i* before *e* except after *c*.
chief   believe   receive

2. Change a final *y* to *i* before adding most endings. But if the word ends in *ay*, *ey*, or *oy*, just add the ending.
country, countries   happy, happily   key, keys

3. Drop a final *e* before adding an ending that begins with *a, e, i, o,* or *u*. If the ending starts with another letter, keep the *e*.
hope, hoping   imagine, imaginary   peace, peaceful

Working It Out

A. Write capital letters above each sentence where they are needed. Cross out the small letters that are wrong.

1. She was reading the *los angeles times* of friday, july 1.

2. Her father, mr. Koros, works for hart paper company.

3. George's uncle fought in the vietnam war.

B. Put in the correct punctuation in each sentence.

1. She worked for Mr T J Orso in Kent Ohio until May 1 1988.

2. Nikki took her coat her purse and her keys with her

3. After we put up the tent for the boys it rained

C. If a word is spelled wrong, write the correct spelling. If it is spelled correctly, write *correct.*

1. countys _____   3. shining _____   5. loveing _____

2. piece _____   4. monkies _____   6. hopful _____

D. If a word is used incorrectly, cross it out. Write the correct word above it.

1. Maurita come to see her father every day.

2. As the sun is setting, we walked back to camp.

3. The store sold out all their sale items.

Looking Ahead

In the next lesson, you'll edit other people's writing. Then you'll get a chance to edit some of your own writing.

Editing Exercises

In this lesson you will
■ practice editing

Getting Started

In the last lesson, you learned some rules for editing your writing. Sometimes it's hard to spot mistakes in your writing. The more you practice editing, the better you become. You can use this list to help you.

Editing Checklist

Did I edit my paragraph for errors in

_____ spelling?   _____ capitalization?

_____ punctuation?   _____ grammar?

Here's an Example

A writer wrote and revised the following paragraph. Then he went back to edit. Here is his paragraph after he edited it.

> My softball ~~teem~~ ^{team} had a ~~grate~~ ^{great} season this year. We ~~was~~ ^{were} the
>
> champions in our league. We had fast ~~pictures~~ ^{pitchers} , hard-hitting
>
> batters , and good ~~feilders~~ ^{fielders}. All the ~~guys~~ ^{players} worked hard to win
>
> Our record was 10 wins and 1 loss Our sponsor, the
>
> ^Mmaplehill ^Ddairy, gave us a big party to celebrate our ~~supper~~ ^{super}
>
> season.

Working It Out

A. The sentences that follow contain errors in capitalization, punctuation, spelling, or grammar. Edit them. Cross out mistakes. Write your corrections in the space above each sentence. Put in punctuation where it's needed.

1. Miss Esther L Lee was born on february 20 1968.

2. Lake huron is peraps the most beutiful of the great lakes.

3. I am hopping that we will see our Friends their.

4. Four silly giggling toddlers was playing in the yard.

5. Dr Hosbach gone to the hospital in a hurry.

B. A student wrote and revised this paragraph but did not edit it. There are capitalization, punctuation, spelling, and grammar mistakes. Read the paragraph carefully. Edit the mistakes by crossing them out and writing corrections above the sentences. Put in punctuation where it's needed.

You often read only about bad people in the news. However there are many good people in our town. Mr Janski is the mayor He works for the scott book company and has his dutys as mayor too. Dr parks take care of the sick men women and children in town The doctor is respected by all who know her. Mrs Osgood is the principle of the school. She is a good freind to the children their Our town, waterford alabama, is a place full of good people.

✏️ Writing On Your Own

Write a paragraph of at least five or six sentences. Your topic is the things that are important to you. Prewrite, write a first draft, and revise. Then edit your paragraph. Use the checklist on page 171 to help you.

_____

_____

_____

_____

_____

_____

GED Challenger

Read this paragraph. Then read the questions that follow. Circle the number of the correction that should be made to each sentence. The sentences have been numbered to help you.

(1) It's not hard to apply for a job at my compeny. (2) First, you go to see mrs. Jones. (3) She will have you fill out some forms. (4) Then you go in and talk to Miss Miles. (5) She will ask you why you want the job. (6) also, she will ask why you should get the job. (7) You need to tell her all the things you can do well. (8) Miss Miles will let you know if you get the job.

1. Sentence 1: **It's not hard to apply for a job at my compeny.**
   What correction should be made to this sentence?
   (1) replace It's with Its
   (2) change the spelling of apply to applie
   (3) put a comma after apply
   (4) change compeny to Compeny
   (5) change the spelling of compeny to company

2. Sentence 2: **First, you go to see mrs. Jones.**
   What correction should be made to this sentence?
   (1) change go to gone
   (2) change go to goes
   (3) replace see with sea
   (4) change mrs. to Mrs.
   (5) change Jones to jones

3. Sentence 6: **also, she will ask why you should get the job.**
   What correction should be made to this sentence?
   (1) change also to Also
   (2) remove the comma after also
   (3) change ask to asked
   (4) change the spelling of should to shood
   (5) change get to have gotten

▲ Looking Back

Editing is an important step in creating a good piece of writing.

Presenting What You Write

> ***In this lesson you will***
> ■ produce the final copy of your writing

Picture It

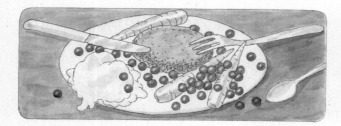 

Which meal appeals to you more? They contain all the same items. However, one is placed in front of you in a much nicer way. It makes you feel that you want to eat it.

When you create a piece of writing, you want to present it in a nice way too. Then your reader will *want* to read it.

Already, you've learned how to do these things:

1. Prewrite
2. Write your first draft
3. Revise
4. Edit

Now there is one more thing you can do. You can present your writing in the best possible way. These tips will help you.

1. Read your paragraph one final time. Read it aloud if possible. Look for words you might make clearer. Look for mistakes you might have missed.

2. Ask someone else to read your paragraph. This person can tell you if some ideas or words are not clear. He or she may also spot a mistake you did not see.

3. Write your paragraph on a sheet of clean, unwrinkled paper. Keep equal space on the left and the right. Write neatly in pen. If you don't write neatly, all your hard work will be wasted. That's because no one will be able to read it! Don't waste your paragraph that way.

Here's an Example

Remember the softball player from the last lesson? He presented this paragraph as his final copy.

My softball team had a great season this year. We were the champions in our league. We had fast pitchers, hard-hitting batters, and good fielders. All the players worked hard to win. Our record was ten wins and one loss. Our sponsor, the Maplehill Dairy, gave us a big party at Angelo's Inn to celebrate our super season.

Working It Out

Here is one woman's paragraph. She has prewritten, written, revised, and edited it. Read it carefully. Are there any words you would change to improve her writing? Are there any mistakes she missed? Then copy it in the space on the next page. Make the final copy look good!

■ Being short sometimes bothers my brother, Aaron. He is little, so many people think he's younger than he is. They don't realize he's a married man with children! Aaron loves basketball, but he is not good at it. He can't jump high enough to make a basket. Aaron says that another bad thing is that he can't reach the cookies in his house. His wife keeps them on the top shelf away from their children. Being short certainly has its problems.

_____
_____
_____
_____
_____
_____
_____

✏️ Writing On Your Own

In the previous lesson you wrote about the important things in your life. Read that paragraph again. Is your writing as good and clear as it can be? Have you edited any mistakes? Ask someone else to read your paragraph. Then write your final copy in the space below.

_____
_____
_____
_____
_____
_____
_____

▲ Looking Back

Once you finish writing, read your paragraph once more. Make sure your message is clear and free from errors. If possible, have someone else read it. Finally, write it neatly in pen on a clean, unwrinkled sheet of paper.

You have finished all your work. Now comes the *best* part. Your reader can finally read your message!

Writing to
Narrate or Describe

Paragraphs That Narrate

In this lesson you will
- read and copy writing that narrates, or tells a story

Picture It

To **narrate** means to tell a story, to tell about something that happened. A story that is narrated might look like this.

Man Bites Dog

Harry Jones, 40, of Walla Walla, Washington, bit his neighbor's dog on the leg when the dog bit Jones's arm and refused to let go.

Or a story can look like this.

Long, long ago,
in a galaxy far away...

Newspaper stories narrate true stories. So do some magazine articles, life stories, letters, and history books. On the other hand, many books, articles, jokes, and even comic strips narrate made-up stories.

Whether true or not, writing that narrates a story is called **narrative writing.**

Here's an Example

An adult student wrote this narrative paragraph. It's a made-up story.

■ Helen Judge walked quickly into the diner. She wanted to have a quick lunch and get back to work. When Helen sat down at the counter, she heard the two men next to her arguing. The next thing she knew, one man was hitting the other. Helen jumped up from her seat. The men moved near her. One took a big punch. He missed the other man and hit Helen right in the eye. Helen fell down. She was knocked out. When Helen came around, she was in the hospital with a black eye and a huge headache!

Another student wrote this true story of events in history.

■ Davy Crockett went to the Alamo fort in San Antonio, Texas. Before long, the Mexican leader, Santa Ana, attacked the fort. Crockett and his men fought hard, but their ammunition ran out. Crockett began to fight with the butt of his rifle. But when the battle was over, Crockett had died with most of his men.

When you want to narrate a story, choose interesting events to tell about. You'll usually put the events in time order, the order in which they happened.

Working It Out

A writer wrote this narrative paragraph to tell about something that happened to him.

■ Yesterday, everything went wrong. I wanted to go shopping. When I started to get into my car, I saw that it had a flat tire! I got out my jack and changed the tire. Then I started to drive down the street. A man in a red sports car pulled out in front of me. I bumped into him. Luckily, his car had only a little scratch. I drove back home and put my car in the garage for the rest of the day!

Sometimes copying a good story helps you see how to write a story of your own. In the space below, copy the story about the bad day in the car.

_____

_____

_____

_____

_____

✏️ *Writing On Your Own*

In Working It Out, the writer narrated some bad events. In the space below, rewrite the paragraph. Make it into a story of *good* events. When you come to each bad event, take it out and put in a good one. You'll end up with a story about a good trip in a car. The first few sentences are written to get you started.

Yesterday, everything was great! I wanted to go shopping. When I started to get into my car, I found some money.

_____

_____

_____

_____

_____

▲ Looking Back

When you write a narrative paragraph, you tell a true or made-up story. You include interesting events. You usually put the events in time order, the order in which they happened.

Prewriting a Narrative Paragraph

> *In this lesson you will*
> ■ think of ideas for a narrative paragraph
> ■ organize ideas for a narrative paragraph

Picture It

Remember when you were a child? Think back to those days. Many pictures probably come to mind.

You can probably tell an interesting story about your childhood. To narrate a story, you need to do some prewriting first. You need to think of ideas, decide on a main idea, and choose details to support it. Then you need to organize your ideas in a map or an outline.

Think of Ideas

Here's an Example

A young man named Matt wanted to write about his childhood. First, he thought of different ideas and memories.

playground   animals   sad
friends   dead bird   hole in garden
pets   summer   box

Matt needed to focus his ideas more. So he asked himself some questions.

WHO: me, bird *WHAT: died, funeral*
WHEN: summer I was 5 *WHERE: my backyard*
WHY: wanted bird to have real funeral
HOW: shoe box coffin, put box in hole in garden

Matt's answers added more details to his list of ideas. They **Discover Main Idea**
gave him a main idea for a story about his childhood. He saw
that most of his ideas were about one thing: the time he buried
a dead bird he had found.

Then Matt chose the details he could use to tell about his **Choose Details**
main idea. He added others as he thought of them.

bluebird died *got box from Mom*
flowers *dug hole* *wrapped bird in paper*

Next, Matt organized these details. He decided to make a map **Organize**
instead of an outline. He put his main idea in the middle of the
map. Then he filled in the rest of the map with his details.

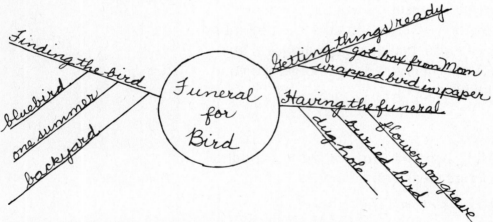

At this point, Matt was ready to write the first draft of his
narrative paragraph.

Working It Out

A mother brainstormed these ideas about a happy event.

| Jim came home | airport | hugs and kisses all around |
| so happy we cried | he's 20 | took family picture |

Then she added some ideas to her list. She asked *who, what, when, where, why,* and *how.*

Who: whole family   *What:* Jim came home
When: last week, early in morning   *Where:* airport
Why: to pick up Jim after two years in Navy
How: felt excited on way out

Look at her ideas. Write what you think is the main idea.

_____

Now check each idea that can be used to explain the main idea. The writer started to make an outline to organize her ideas. Complete the outline for her. Use ideas from the details you checked.

1. _____

    a.   whole family left early

    b.   excited on the way out

2. Jim arrived

    a.   _____

    b.   so happy we cried

    c.   _____

✏️ *Writing On Your Own*

Choose a story you want to tell. It can be something that happened to you. It can be a story you've read or seen on TV or in the movies. On your own paper, jot down all the ideas about the story you can think of.

You may want to ask yourself *who, what, when, where, why,* and *how* about the story.

Now look at your ideas. What main idea comes to your mind? Write your main idea.

Check each idea you can use to explain your main idea. Add more ideas if you can. These will be the supporting details in your story.

You're now ready to organize your ideas. You can decide if you want to outline or map your story ideas.

▲ Looking Back

To narrate a story, you first need to prewrite. Think of ideas, discover your main idea, choose supporting details, and make an outline or a map. Now you're ready to write your first draft.

Drafting a Narrative Paragraph

> *In this lesson you will*
> - write the first draft of a narrative paragraph

Getting Started

Remember Matt from the previous lesson? He wanted to tell the story about burying the dead bird. He drew a map that looked like this.

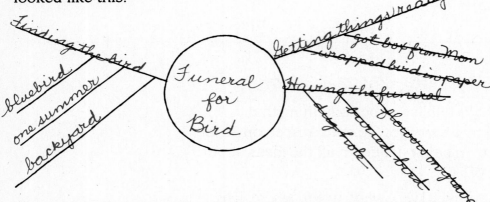

Then Matt started to write the first draft of his story. First he put his main idea in a sentence. His main idea was about burying a dead bird. He used the idea to write this topic sentence: *It seems almost silly to me now, but the day I buried a dead bird was a very sad day of my childhood.*

   Next, Matt wrote the other sentences in his story. He used the details from his map to write them. He put the details in the order in which they happened.

Here's an Example

The first draft of Matt's narrative paragraph looked like this. Note the topic sentence at the beginning. See how the details are ordered.

- It seems almost silly to me now, but the day I buried a dead bird was a very sad day of my childhood. I found the dead bluebird in my backyard one summer. I felt sad about it, so I asked my mother for a box. She didn't know what the box was for. I wrapped the bird in paper and put it in the box. Next, I dug a hole in the yard and buried the box in it. I even put flowers on the bird's grave! I was only five, but something about the bird affected me. I remember the "funeral" to this day.

Working It Out

A mother was another writer in Lesson 23. She made this outline for a narrative paragraph about a happy event.

Jim's return was happy.
1. Trip to the airport
      whole family left early
      excited on the way out
2. Jim arrived
      hugs and kisses all around
      so happy we cried
      took a family picture

The main idea for her paragraph is that Jim's return was a happy event. Write a topic sentence for the paragraph below.

_____

The mother started to write her first draft. Finish it for her. Use the details from the outline above in the sentences you write. Keep the actions in time order.

- The whole family left home at 5 A.M. to go to the airport. We were all excited. We hadn't seen Jim in two years. His plane arrived at 7:30. When he got off the plane,

_____

_____

_____

_____

✏️ *Writing On Your Own*

Look again at the outline or map you made for Writing on Your Own in Lesson 23. It tells a story that happened to you or one you've read or seen.

Now write the main idea of your story in a sentence. This will be the topic sentence of your narrative paragraph.

_____

Next, write the other sentences in your paragraph. Use the details from your outline or map. Put the details in time order. In the space below, copy your topic sentence first. Then write the rest of your first draft. Remember: A first draft does *not* have to be perfect. You'll revise and edit your paragraph later.

_____
_____
_____
_____
_____
_____
_____
_____
_____

▲ Looking Back

For the first draft of a narrative paragraph, look at your main idea. Write it in a topic sentence. Then use your details to write the other sentences. Put your details in time order.

Revising and Editing a Narrative Paragraph

> *In this lesson you will*
> - revise a narrative paragraph
> - edit a narrative paragraph

Getting Started

Here's the first draft of one writer's narrative paragraph. She writes about her first subway ride as a child.

- My frist ride on the subway. When my mother and I walked down into the subway station, people kept pushing us. They were all rushing to the train. The train came. I stepped on. I thought the door would close on me. The subway started. It moved so fast. I thought we would crash. My mother held on to me, but I was scarred. I was glad when that trip was over!

The writer has some things wrong. For example, she doesn't have a complete topic sentence. Also, some sentences are short and choppy. That's OK because this is her first draft. Now she'll revise her paragraph. She'll read it several times to see if she can improve it. She can use the following checklist.

Revising Checklist

_____ **1.** Have I stated my main idea clearly in a topic sentence?

_____ **2.** Do my details support my main idea?

_____ **3.** Have I included specific facts, examples, and reasons to explain my details?

_____ **4.** Are my details written in a clear order?

_____ **5.** Have I left out any important ideas?

_____ **6.** Did I connect my ideas with linking words?

_____ **7.** Did I use a variety of sentences?

_____ **8.** Did I use specific, concise words?

The writer also knows she has a few mistakes in her paragraph. After revising, she edits her narrative paragraph. This checklist helps her.

Editing Checklist

Did I edit my paragraph for errors in

_____ **1.** capitalization?

_____ **2.** punctuation?

_____ **3.** spelling?

_____ **4.** grammar?

Here's an Example

See how the woman has revised and edited her first draft below.

My ~~frist~~ *first* ride on the subway. *scared me.* When my mother and I walked down into the subway station, people kept pushing us. They were all rushing to the train. *Then* The train came. *When* I stepped on. I thought the door would close on me. The subway started. *and* It moved so fast. I thought we would crash. My mother held on to me, but I was ~~scarred~~ *scared*. I was glad when that trip was over!

The writer completed her topic sentence. She combined sentences to add variety to them. She also edited some spelling and punctuation mistakes.

Working It Out

Here's a narrative paragraph about a happy event. The writer has not revised or edited it. Use the checklist on page 187 to revise the paragraph. You may need to read the paragraph several times to check all the points. Then use the checklist on page 188 to edit the paragraph. Write your changes and corrections between the lines.

■ I got up erly and put on my best suit. This was last Friday, which was a very good day for me. I drove to the Beekman Printing company. I went to see Mr. J K Beekman in his office. He talked to me about a new job opening. I told him that I could run a press and manage people. He like what I had to say about what I could do. Mr. Beekman offered me a job. What a grate day it turned out to be!

Writing On Your Own

In the previous lesson, you wrote about a story you read, saw, or lived through. Go back to that paragraph now. Use the checklist on page 187 to help you revise your narrative. Read it over several times to cover all the points. Then edit your paragraph. Use the editing checklist on page 188. Once you've revised and edited, copy your paragraph below. Present it in the best possible way.

_____

_____

_____

_____

_____

▲ Looking Back

After you finish the first draft of a narrative paragraph, you need to revise it. Make sure your main idea and details are clear and well written. Then you want to edit it for any errors. Last, rewrite your paragraph in clear handwriting.

Paragraphs That Describe

In this lesson you will
■ read and copy writing that describes

Picture It

To **describe** means to give a picture, in words, of a person, place, or thing. To do this, a good writer uses specific words. A specific word shows the reader how something looks, sounds, tastes, smells, or feels. The words appeal to the reader's five senses. A writer might use these words to describe the pictures below.

salty smell
splashing
hot, gritty sand
colorful umbrellas

yellow hard hat
rough hands
dirty blue jeans
sweaty

silky
striped
loose fitting
ruffled

Writing that describes is called **descriptive writing.** When you write a descriptive paragraph, tell about as many senses as you can. Here are some specific words you can use to describe things.

Looks	Sounds	Tastes	Smells	Feels
bumpy	whisper	tangy	fresh	rough
curly	whining	salty	lemony	velvety
green	squeak	sweet	sweaty	silky
round	roar	bitter	musty	slippery
tiny	tapping	sour	smoky	icy

Here's an Example

A man described a beautiful woman he met.

- Elizabeth was a beautiful woman. Her black hair was long and silky. She had deep brown eyes and long black eyelashes. Elizabeth's skin was smooth and tanned. A little pink lipstick and gray eye shadow was the only make-up she had on. Her perfume smelled like roses. She wore a soft, fuzzy, white sweater and a black skirt. She really caught my eye.

You can picture Elizabeth from that description, can't you? Another man described a pot of tomato sauce.

- The huge black pot sat on the stove. Bubbling sounds came from inside. Clouds of steam puffed out from the top of the pot. Inside, hot tomato sauce cooked slowly. The deep red sauce had tiny specks of green pepper floating on the top. I saw chunks of brown meat in there too. The smell of sweet tomatoes and hot meat filled the kitchen.

Could you see, hear, and smell the tomato sauce?

Working It Out

A writer wrote this paragraph to describe a place in the woods.

- The log cabin stood among tall, green pine trees. Smoke curled from the gray stone chimney. The smell of burning wood mixed with the fragrance of pine. Beside the cabin, a stream ran down the hill, splashing over rocks. The water sparkled in the bright sunshine. This was a place to feel good.

The writer used specific words to make you see ("green pine," "smoke curled," "stream ran," "water sparkled"). She wrote "splashing" to make you hear the sound of the stream. The words "smell of burning wood" and "fragrance of pine" make you smell the place.

Sometimes copying a description helps you see how to write one of your own. In the space below, copy the paragraph that describes the place in the woods.

_____

_____

_____

_____

_____

Writing On Your Own

In "Working It Out," the writer described a place in the woods. In the spaces below, rewrite the paragraph. This time describe a place in a town. Describe a building and the space around it. Give word pictures of the sights, smells, and sounds.

_____

_____

_____

_____

▲ Looking Back

When you write a descriptive paragraph, give the reader a "word picture" of a person, place, or thing. Use specific words that help your reader see, hear, taste, smell, or feel.

Prewriting a Descriptive Paragraph

In this lesson you will
- think of ideas for a descriptive paragraph
- organize ideas for a descriptive paragraph

Picture It

In the previous lesson, you read examples of descriptive writing. To write your own descriptive paragraph, begin by prewriting. You first need ideas that describe someone or something.

How do you find ideas that help you describe? People understand the world through their five senses. They see, hear, taste, smell, and touch.

See   **Hear**   **Taste**   **Smell**   **Touch**

To prewrite for a descriptive paragraph, first use your senses. How does the person, place, or thing look, sound, taste, smell, or feel? List as many ideas as you can. Be as specific as you can.

Once you've listed ideas, look at them. Decide on a main idea. Then choose the details you can use to tell about the main idea. Add more details if you can. Next, organize your ideas in an outline or a map. Then you're ready to start your first draft.

Here's an Example

A student wanted to describe a pizza.

First, he used his senses. He thought of what a pizza looks, smells, tastes, sounds, and feels like. He jotted down these ideas.

Think of Ideas

Looks	Smells	Tastes	Sounds	Feels
red sauce	spicy	hot	sizzles	hot
white cheese	cheesy	spicy		gooey
round crust	from oven	crispy		
pieces				

Next, the writer looked at his ideas. He discovered that most of them made a pizza good to eat. That became his main idea.

Discover Main Idea

Then, he decided what details he would use to describe the pizza. He tried to add details too.

Choose Details

Finally, he made a map of his ideas. His map looked like this.

Organize

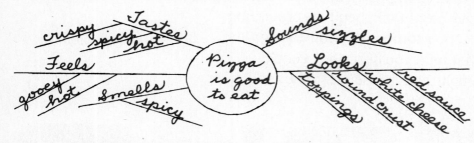

Now the writer was ready to begin his first draft.

Working It Out

A father thought of these ideas to describe his baby.

Happy		Sad or mad	
coos	blue eyes light up	wiggly	puffed cheeks
milk	powdery smell	reddish	teary cheeks
hums	pinkish glow	sobs	shrill cry
smiles	cuddly	hurts	

Look at his list of ideas. Write the main idea for a paragraph that has many of these ideas.

_____

Now check all the ideas that tell about the main idea. They will be supporting details.

The writer then started to outline his ideas. Complete this outline for him with ideas from his list.

When she's happy
1. Looks
   pinkish glow

   _____
   _____
2. Sounds

   _____
   _____
3. Feels
   cuddly

When she's sad or mad
1. Looks
   reddish

   _____

   puffed cheeks
2. Sounds
   sobs

   _____
3. Feels
   wiggly

Writing On Your Own

Choose a person *you* want to describe. First, jot down ideas. Use your senses to help you.

Looks   **Smells**   **Sounds**   **Feels**

What main idea comes to mind when you look at your ideas? Write your main idea.

_____

Now check each idea you can use to tell about your main idea. Add details if you can. These will be the supporting details.

You're ready now to organize your ideas. Make an outline or a map of your details on your own paper.

▲ Looking Back

To describe a person, place, or thing, you need to prewrite. First, think of ideas that will appeal to your reader's five senses. Next, decide on a main idea. Then, choose supporting details. Finally, make an outline or a map to organize your ideas. Then you're ready to write a good first draft.

Drafting a Descriptive Paragraph

In this lesson you will
- write the first draft of a descriptive paragraph

Getting Started

In the previous lesson, you thought of ideas for a descriptive paragraph. Now you'll use those ideas to write a first draft.

Remember the writer in that lesson who wanted to describe the pizza? His map looked like this:

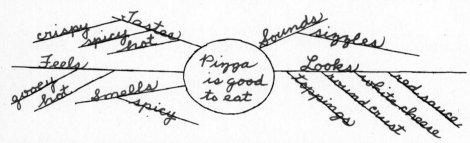

To start his first draft, he put his main idea in a sentence. He wrote this: *A pizza is a mouthwatering treat throughout.* Next, he used the details from his map to write the other sentences.

Here's an Example

The writer's first draft looked like this. As you read, note the order he used for his details. He described the pizza from the outside in.

- A pizza is a mouthwatering treat throughout. A round, crisp crust rims the outside. Then a ring of spicy red tomato sauce sizzles. Within the middle lies hot, gooey white cheese over the sauce. Bits and pieces of juicy meat and vegetables top it. No wonder the whole pizza is good to eat.

The writer put his supporting details in a **space order.** He described how the pizza looks from the outside to the inside. You can use space order to describe other things. For example, you can write about a room from left to right. Or you can describe a person from the top of his head to the tip of his toes.

Working It Out

Here's the outline a man made to describe his baby.

My Baby's Different Moods
When she's happy
1. Looks
   pinkish glow
   smiles
   blue eyes light up
2. Sounds
   coos
   hums
3. Feels
   cuddly

When she's sad or mad
1. Looks
   reddish
   teary cheeks
   puffed cheeks
2. Sounds
   sobs
   shrill cry
3. Feels
   wiggly

The topic sentence is going to tell about the baby's different moods. Write a good topic sentence for the paragraph.

_____

The writer started his first draft. He described his baby when she was happy. Then he began to contrast that by describing an unhappy baby. You learned about comparing and contrasting in Lesson 14 in Part B. When you compare and contrast, you show how things are alike and different.

Finish writing the man's contrast for him. Use the details from the outline that show how different the baby is when she's sad or mad.

When Elizabeth is happy, her blue eyes light up. Her whole face has a pinkish glow. She flashes a toothless smile at you. Then she coos and hums so softly that she makes you smile. She feels so cuddly then. However, when Elizabeth is sad or mad,

_____

_____

_____

_____ But I love her no matter what mood she's in.

✏️ Writing On Your Own

Look again at the outline or map you made for Writing on Your Own in the previous lesson. It describes a person you know.
    Write the main idea of your outline or map in a sentence. Write a good topic sentence for your paragraph.

_____

    Next, use your details to write the other sentences in the paragraph. You may want to put the details in space order (top to bottom). You may compare and contrast the person at different times. Or you may just want to order your details by the senses they tell about: looks, sounds, smells, and feels. Copy your topic sentence first. Then write the rest of your first draft. Remember: Your first draft does not have to be perfect.

_____

_____

_____

▲ Looking Back

For the first draft of a descriptive paragraph, look at your main idea. Put it in a topic sentence. Then use your details to write the other sentences. Put your details in space order, compare and contrast them, or group them by senses.

Revising and Editing a Descriptive Paragraph

In this lesson you will
- revise a descriptive paragraph
- edit a descriptive paragraph

Picture It

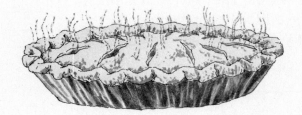

In Lesson 28 you worked with first drafts of descriptive paragraphs. Now you'll revise and edit some first drafts.

Here is the first draft of one writer's paragraph. She describes a food she really likes.

- Hot apple pie has to be the best dessert in the world. The lite brown crust covers the apples it has been pushed down with a fork to make little marks around the outside of the pie plate. Little puffs of steam come out. Tiny wholes in the top of the crust have hot apple juice running out of them. The golden apple slises are covered with sugar. you take a bite, the sweet apples and flaky crust tastes great.

The writer's first draft has a few problems. She'll read it several times to revise it.

Like many writers, the woman has errors in spelling and grammar. She also has sentences that run on. Once she's revised her paragraph, she'll edit it for these errors.

Here's an Example

This is the writer's paragraph after she revised and then edited it. She used the checklists in the margin to help her. They are shortened forms of the checklists on pages 187–188. If you need to review the exact questions, look back at those pages.

pages 187–188

Hot apple pie has to be the best dessert in the world. The ~~lite~~ *light* brown crust ~~covers~~ *hides* the apples. *I* ~~i~~t has been ~~pushed down~~ *indented* with a fork ~~to make little marks~~ *all* around the outside of the pie plate. Little puffs of steam come out*, too* ⁀ Tiny ~~wholes~~ *holes* in the top of the crust ~~have~~ *ooze* hot apple juice ~~running out of them.~~ The golden apple ~~slices~~ *slices* are covered with *a syrup of white* sugar*, and brown cinnamon.* *Y*ou take a bite · *T*~~t~~he sweet*, tangy* apples and flaky crust tastes great.

> **Revise for—**
> _____ Main idea
> _____ Supporting details
> _____ Facts, examples, and reasons
> _____ Clear order
> _____ Missing ideas
> _____ Linking words
> _____ Sentence variety
> _____ Specific, concise words

The woman moved one sentence to make the order of details clearer. She added many specific words. They give you a much better picture of the pie. Also, she edited her spelling and grammar mistakes. Finally, she fixed sentences by adding the right end punctuation—periods.

> **Edit for—**
> _____ Capitalization
> _____ Punctuation
> _____ Spelling
> _____ Grammar

An Idea to Remember

You revise first, and then you edit. Yet sometimes you'll catch a mistake when you're revising. Or you may want to revise a sentence when you're editing. That's all right to do. Good writers sometimes go back and forth a little between writing steps. But don't try to revise and edit together. You'll end up with a paragraph that is not well revised or well edited.

Working It Out

Here's a descriptive paragraph about a street corner. It needs revising and then editing. Read it through first. Then revise it using the checklist above. Read it several times to cover all the points on the list. Finally, edit the paragraph. Use the checklist above to help you.

■ Standing on the corner of broad street and third avenue is intresting. People in heavy winter coats, scarves, and gloves rush by. People bump into each other and mumble "Excuse me" or "Sorry." Big blue buses stop. People pile out. Bus fumes fill the air. A shiny silver pretzel cart is there. A man in a blue snowsuit stands beside it. The salty yeasty smell of pretzels goes through the air. The hum of car and bus engines and the honking of horns is loud at this busy spot

Writing On Your Own

Go back now to the descriptive paragraph you wrote in Lesson 28. Revise it to make your description clear and specific. Read it several times to make sure you've revised it well. Use the checklist on pages 187–188 to help you cover all the points. Next, edit your paragraph for mistakes. The checklist on page 188 will help you. Finally, rewrite your paragraph here in easy-to-read handwriting.

_____

_____

_____

_____

_____

▲ Looking Back

After you finish the first draft of a descriptive paragraph, you need to revise it. Then you need to edit it for mistakes. Finally, you can rewrite it in clear handwriting to present to your reader.

Writing to Explain or Persuade

Paragraphs That Explain

> *In this lesson you will*
> ■ read and copy writing that explains

Picture It

Explanatory writing is writing that explains, informs, or gives directions. Some examples of explanatory writing might look like this.

Explanatory writing is interesting to read *and* to write.

Here's an Example

An insurance saleswoman wrote this paragraph. It explains insurance rates.

■ People often complain about higher insurance rates, but there are reasons the rates go up. For example, take car insurance. If you're in an accident, your rates will go up. That's because the insurance company has paid money to fix your car. Perhaps *you* are not in an accident, but many other people are. Then the company will raise your rates to help it pay to fix other people's cars. Or perhaps car repair shops start charging more for their work. Then the insurance company will raise your rates because it has to pay more. You may not like these reasons. However, they help you see *why* you are paying more for insurance.

The paragraph explains why insurance rates go up. It lists several reasons for higher rates. Accidents and higher repair costs are *causes.* The higher rates are the *effects.* Explanatory paragraphs often deal with such cause-and-effect relationships. You read and wrote about causes and effects in Lesson 13 in Part B.

Working It Out

A bank teller wrote this paragraph to explain how to write a check. He wrote it in **step-by-step order.** This is similar to time order. He wrote the steps in the same order as you would do them.

■ Writing a check is not a hard thing to do. First, you write the date in the upper right-hand corner of the check. Next, you write the name of the person or company you are paying after the words "Pay to the order of." After the dollar sign, you write the amount you want to pay in numbers. Then you write this same amount in words in front of the word "Dollars." Finally, you sign your full name in the lower right-hand corner of the check. Then the check is ready to give to the person you are paying.

Sometimes copying an explanatory paragraph helps you see how to write one of your own. In the space below and on the next page, copy the paragraph explaining how to write a check.

_____

_____

_____

_____

_____

_____

_____

_____

_____

✏️➡ *Writing On Your Own*

In Working It Out, the writer explained how to write a check. In the spaces below, explain how to do something else. Maybe you could explain how to change a car tire, how to bake a cake, or how to get from your house to the supermarket. Put your ideas in step-by-step order.

_____

_____

_____

_____

_____

_____

_____

_____

_____

▲ Looking Back

When you write an explanatory paragraph, you explain, inform on a topic, or give directions on how to do something. You put your ideas in a clear order that shows how they are related. Causes and effects and steps in a process are just two kinds of ways to organize your ideas when you do explanatory writing.

Prewriting an Explanatory Paragraph

In this lesson you will
■ think of ideas for an explanatory paragraph
■ organize ideas for an explanatory paragraph

Picture It

Have you ever been asked for directions? If so, details like these probably came to mind.

When you want to write directions or other information, you want to write an explanatory paragraph. In Lesson 30 you read about explanatory writing. In this lesson, you'll think of ideas for a paragraph that explains.

Explanatory writing is just like other writing. You first need to prewrite. Think of ideas by brainstorming, or by asking questions, or both. Discover your main idea. Choose the details that best tell about your main idea. Finally, organize your details by making an outline or a map. You're then ready to start your first draft.

Here's an Example

A student named Al worked in a health club. He wanted to write a paragraph explaining sweat. First he jotted down ideas for the paragraph.

Think of Ideas

everyone sweats   good for you   normal body heat
work   hot body   can kill you   feel damp
cool off   feel cooler   heat in sweat   sweat into air

Next, Al looked at his ideas. He decided the main idea of his paragraph would explain why people sweat.

Discover Main Idea

Then he checked off details from his list he could use to explain why people sweat. He added a few details too.

Choose Details

Finally, Al made an outline of his ideas. He saw that his details were both causes and effects. His outline looked like this.

Organize

Why People Sweat

1. Causes
   body makes heat
   sun heats body
   work makes more heat
2. Effects
   body can get too hot (can kill you)
   sweat comes out of skin
   takes heat out of body
   body feels cooler

Al was ready to write a first draft that explains why people sweat.

Working It Out

A job counselor brainstormed these ideas about jobs.

friendly co-workers	hard to find	vacation time	interesting
Mom works	near home	promotions	good boss

Then she added some ideas to the list by asking questions.

Who: person looking for job   *What:* good pay, insurance, raises
When: Monday through Friday   *Where:* clean, safe building
Why: to support family   *How:* ads, contacts

Look at the list of ideas. Write the main idea suggested by the details.

_____

Now check the ideas that could be used to tell about the main idea.

Next, fill in the map the writer started to organize her ideas. Use ideas from the list.

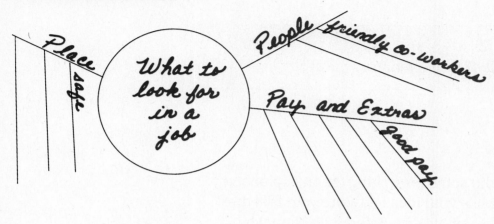

✏️➤ *Writing On Your Own*

Choose a sport or an activity you enjoy. It could be camping, bowling, car racing, sewing, gardening, basketball, hiking, or swimming. You might like doing it or just watching. Explain this sport or activity in a paragraph.

First, brainstorm some ideas about the sport or activity. Or ask yourself *who, what, when, where, why,* and *how.* Or do both.

Think of Ideas

What main idea comes to mind when you look at your ideas? Write the main idea.

Discover Main Idea

Now check each idea you can use to tell about your main idea. Add details if you can.

Choose Details

Finally, make an outline or a map to organize your ideas.

Organize

▲ Looking Back

When you write an explanatory paragraph, prewrite first. Brainstorm or ask questions to come up with ideas. Next, look at your ideas and decide on a main idea. Then choose the details that will tell about your main idea. Finally, make an outline or a map to organize your ideas. If you follow these steps, you'll be ready to write your first draft.

Drafting an Explanatory Paragraph

In this lesson you will
- write the first draft of an explanatory paragraph

Getting Started

In the last lesson you did some prewriting for an explanatory paragraph. Now you'll use your ideas to write your first draft.

Al was a writer in Lesson 31. He wanted to explain why people sweat. His outline looked like this.

Why People Sweat

1. Causes
   body makes heat
   sun heats body
   work makes more heat

2. Effects
   body can get too hot (can kill you)
   sweat comes out of skin
   takes heat out of body
   body feels cooler

Al started to write the first draft of his paragraph. He put his main idea in a sentence. He wrote this topic sentence: *People need to sweat to keep cool.*

Next, Al used the details from his outline. They became the other sentences in his paragraph. He wrote about the causes and effects of sweat.

Here's an Example

Al's explanatory paragraph looks like this.

- People need to sweat to keep cool. Your body makes heat. When you exercise, your body makes even more heat. The sun also heats up your body. But your body can get too hot. Too much heat can even kill you. So water comes out of your skin. This sweat takes extra heat out of your body. Once the sweat goes into the air, your body feels cool. This is why people sweat.

Al explained the causes of sweat. Then he told the effects that sweating has on your body.

> **An Idea to Remember**
>
> You can use linking words to show how your ideas are related in an explanatory paragraph. You can review those words in Lesson 16 of Part B.

Working It Out

A job counselor was writing an explanatory paragraph in Lesson 31. The paragraph is about things to look for in a job. Here's a map for her paragraph.

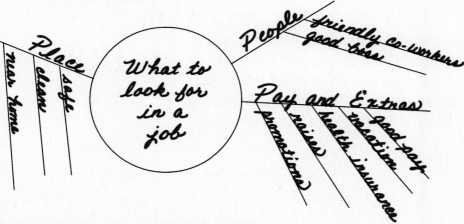

Write a topic sentence for the paragraph.

_____

The counselor started to write her first draft. She began to put the details from the map in sentences. She wrote them in order of importance. Her first details are the most important things about a job. Complete the paragraph for her. Use the details from the map in the sentences you write. Continue putting them in order of importance.

■ Of course, you want a job that's interesting. Aside from that, you should look for a job that pays well. You also want to be able to be promoted and earn raises. You want some extras too. You want health insurance and at least two weeks' vacation each year. After pay and extras, you need to look for a good place to work.

_____

_____

_____

✏️➤ *Writing On Your Own*

Look at the outline or map you made for Writing on Your Own in Lesson 31. It tells about a sport or activity that you enjoy.

Put the main idea of your outline or map into a sentence. Write a good topic sentence for your explanatory paragraph.

_____

Next, use the details from your outline or map to write the other sentences in your first draft. Decide how they are related. Are they steps in a process? Are they reasons you can list in order of importance? Are they causes and effects? Perhaps your ideas are related in some other way. Write them in an order that clearly shows how they are related.

_____

_____

_____

_____

▲ Looking Back

For the first draft of an explanatory paragraph, put your main idea in a topic sentence. Then use your details to write the other sentences. Put your details in an order that makes their relationship clear.

Revising and Editing an Explanatory Paragraph

> *In this lesson you will*
> ■ revise an explanatory paragraph
> ■ edit an explanatory paragraph

Getting Started

Here's the first draft of one writer's paragraph. It explains why people get thirsty.

> ■ Your body is full of salt water. So you get thirsty at some time. You have some amounts of the salt and the water in your body all the time. When you eat to much salt, your body has too much salt and not enough water. When you sweat alot, your body will have too much salt and not enough water. Your body makes you feel thirsty. You drink water, your body gets back to its normal levels of salt and water, you dont feel thirsty anymore.

You know that a first draft is never perfect. It always needs revising and editing. The paragraph above has an unclear main idea. There are few linking words to show the relationship between ideas. Also, there are spelling and punctuation mistakes. The writer knew she had to revise and edit her paragraph.

Here's an Example

The writer used the first checklist in the margin to revise her paragraph. Then she edited it with the help of the second checklist. Review the long forms of the checklists on pages 187–188 if you need to. Then see how the writer revised and edited her paragraph.

Review the long forms of the checklists on pages 187–188 if you need to.

~~The reason is that~~ *Why do*
(~~Your body is full of salt water.~~) ~~So~~ you get thirsty ~~at~~ some
time*s?* ~~^~~ You have some amounts of ~~the~~ salt and ~~the~~ water in
your body all the time. When you eat ~~to~~ *too* much salt, ~~your body~~
~~has too much salt and not enough water~~. ~~W~~When you sweat
a lot
~~alot~~, your body will have too much salt and not enough
When that happens, *If*
water. ~~Your~~ body makes you feel thirsty. ~~^~~ You drink water,
Then
your body gets back to its normal levels of salt and water. ~~^~~ you
don't feel thirsty anymore.

The writer revised her first two sentences to make her main idea clear. She started with a question to help vary her sentences. She added linking words to show the causes and effects. And, of course, she edited her spelling and fixed her sentence punctuation.

Revise for—
_____ Main idea
_____ Supporting details
_____ Facts, examples, and reasons
_____ Clear order
_____ Missing ideas
_____ Linking words
_____ Sentence variety
_____ Specific, concise words

Edit for—
_____ Capitalization
_____ Punctuation
_____ Spelling
_____ Grammar

Working It Out

Here's another explanatory paragraph that needs revising and editing. Use the short checklists on this page or the long checklists on pages 187–188 to help you. Write your changes and corrections in the spaces between the lines.

Use the short checklists on this page or the long checklists on pages 187–188 to help you.

■ Playing cards is something my friends and me like to do. Jo Jane, Bill Madsen Pete Judge and I play cards every friday night. It's a good way to spend free time. It's relaxing. We laugh and try to beet each other at the game. It is also a good way to make our minds work. We try to figure a way to win. We try to figure out the cards the other players has in their hands. Playing cards is a good way to get together.

Writing On Your Own

Turn back to the paragraph you wrote in Lesson 32 about a sport or an activity. Revise your paragraph carefully. Then edit it for mistakes. Use the short checklists on page 214 or the long checklists on pages 187–188 to help you. Finally, rewrite your explanatory paragraph in good handwriting.

_____

_____

_____

_____

_____

_____

GED Challenger

On the GED Test, you must write an explanatory essay. The topic is given on the test. It might be something like this.

> Many people spend a great deal of time watching TV. Television programs are shown 24 hours a day. There are hundreds of TV stations to watch.
>
> Why is watching television such a popular way to spend free time? Explain your answer to this question. Give specific reasons.

On your own paper, write an explanatory paragraph to answer the essay question. Don't forget to prewrite, write a first draft, revise, and then edit.

▲ Looking Back

After you write the first draft of an explanatory paragraph, be sure to revise and then edit it.

Paragraphs That Persuade

> *In this lesson you will*
> ■ read and copy writing that persuades

Picture It

To **persuade** means to try to get readers to think as you do or to act as you want them to. A piece of writing that persuades is called **persuasive writing.** Persuasive writing can look like this.

VOTE FOR MANUEL CRUZ

Manuel will get a
child-care center built here.
Manuel will get
better garbage pickup.
He will make this
a better place to live.
Manuel Cruz will help
all of us.

The Denver Times

Keeping Our Children Drug-Free

You can help keep drugs from your children. Talk to your children about the horrible effects drugs can have. Even more important, find rewarding activities for them to do in their free time. Let them know you are there to talk anytime.

To persuade a reader, you state your ideas about a topic. Then you give facts, reasons, and examples to show your ideas are correct. You use details that could change your reader's way of thinking.

Here's an Example

An adult student was bothered by smoke in a restaurant. He wrote the following paragraph to persuade the owner to ban smoking. He put his least important idea first and his most important idea last.

- Please ban smoking in your restaurant. The smell of smoke sticks to people's clothes. The smoke spoils the taste of your fine food. Even more serious, smoking is dangerous. A person could drop a cigarette or match and start a fire. Most important of all, the smoke hurts people's lungs. Just breathing others' smoke can cause lung cancer, which leads to death. Help all your customers by stopping smoking in your restaurant.

When a writer wants to persuade, he or she often puts the ideas in order of importance. As a writer, you can put the most important ideas first and the least important ones last. Or you can write them the other way around.

Working It Out

A writer wrote this persuasive paragraph. He was trying to persuade his neighbors to clean up their neighborhood.

- Our neighborhood needs a good clean-up. Many houses look run-down. There is litter on the sidewalks and in the streets. Some fences and walls have been spray-painted. If we all work together, we can make things look better. We could form a Clean-Up Group that works on weekends. Think how pleasant it would be to come home to a clean neighborhood each night. You would be proud to live here. You would be able to enjoy walking down the street and sitting on your front porch. Let's work together to make this a good place to live.

The writer states his opinion. Then he gives examples of how the neighborhood looks. Next, he gives reasons for working together to change how it looks. He tries to persuade his readers to clean up their neighborhood.

Sometimes copying a good persuasive paragraph helps you see how to write one of your own. On the lines that follow, copy the paragraph persuading the readers to clean up their neighborhood.

_____

_____

_____

_____

_____

_____

_____

_____

✏️➤ *Writing On Your Own*

In Working It Out, the writer persuaded his readers to clean up their neighborhood. The clean-up would improve their way of life. In the spaces below, persuade a person to do something that will improve his or her way of life. You might persuade someone to stop smoking, to study for the GED Test, or to go on a diet. State your idea. Then give reasons to support it.

_____

_____

_____

_____

_____

_____

▲ Looking Back

When you write a persuasive paragraph, you try to get your reader to think the way you do or to act in a certain way. You state your opinion and then back it up with reasons, facts, or examples.

Prewriting a Persuasive Paragraph

> **In this lesson you will**
> ■ think of ideas for a persuasive paragraph
> ■ organize ideas for a persuasive paragraph

Picture It

When you were a child, did you always do what your parents wanted? Probably not. Most children don't. But there were things that usually persuaded you to obey. Some of them are pictured below. If you're a parent, you probably "persuade" your own child in these ways.

When you want to persuade someone in writing, you need to think of ideas. These ideas should make your reader want to change his or her mind. Then decide what your main idea seems to be. Choose the details that support your main idea. Next, organize your details by making an outline or a map. Then you will be ready to write your first draft of a persuasive paragraph.

Here's an Example

A student named Ella wanted to persuade her brother to learn to read. She asked herself questions to get ideas to persuade him. She was going to write a persuasive letter to her sister-in-law.

Think of Ideas

Who: my brother   What: learn to read
When: good to read anytime
Where: helpful to read everywhere
How: adult ed classes   Why: get better job,
make more money, feel better, be proud, read newspaper,
learn more, understand directions, feel smarter,

Ella looked at her ideas. She decided her main idea was that learning to read helps in more than one way. Then she decided what details she would use to support the main idea. She tried to add details. Finally, she made this outline.

Discover Main Idea

Choose Details

Learn to Read
1. Feel better about yourself
   be proud
   feel smarter

2. Helps in daily life
   understand directions
   read newspaper
   get a better job
   make more money

Organize

Finally, Ella was ready to begin her first draft.

Working It Out

One writer brainstormed these ideas about drinking and driving.

horrible effects   lose control   kill others   kill self
react more slowly   can't see well   cause suffering
hurt others   cripple yourself   should lose license

Look at the list of ideas. Write what you think the main idea is.

Now check all the ideas that can be used to tell about the main idea. These will be the supporting details.

    Next, complete the map the writer started. Use ideas from the list.

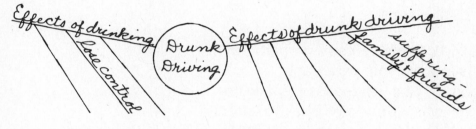

Writing On Your Own

Suppose you want to persuade someone to give you a job. On your own paper, list ideas that you might use. Brainstorm or ask yourself the questions *who, what, when, where, why,* and *how.*

Think of Ideas

What main idea do many of your ideas have in common? Write the main idea down.

Discover Main Idea

Now check each idea you can use to tell about your main idea. Add more details if you can.

Choose Details

Finally, make an outline or a map to organize your ideas.

Organize

▲ Looking Back

To prewrite for a persuasive paragraph, brainstorm or ask questions to come up with ideas. Next, decide on a main idea. Think who your reader will be. Then choose the details that will persuade the reader. Last, organize your ideas with a map or an outline.

Drafting a Persuasive Paragraph

> **In this lesson you will**
> - write the first draft of a persuasive paragraph

Getting Started

In Lesson 35 you thought of ideas for a persuasive paragraph. Now you'll use those ideas to write your paragraph.

Remember Ella in Lesson 35? She wanted to persuade her brother to learn to read. She was writing a persuasive letter for her sister-in-law to read to him. Her outline looked like this.

Learn to Read
1. Feel better about yourself
   be proud
   feel smarter
2. Helps in daily life
   understand directions
   read newspaper
   get a better job
   make more money

Ella started to write her first draft. Her main idea was about learning to read. She used the idea to write this topic sentence: *You really should learn to read.*

Next, she used the details in her outline to write the other sentences in her paragraph.

Here's an Example

The first draft of Ella's paragraph looked like this.

- You really should learn to read. If you can read, you will feel better about yourself. You will be proud that you learned to read. You will feel smarter. That will make you happy. Being able to read will also help you in your daily life. When you can read, you can get a better job and earn more money. You will also be able to understand words in books, on boxes, and on signs. When you come home at night, you will be able to sit down and read the newspaper. Think about learning to read. I'm glad I did.

Ella listed the reasons for learning to read. She felt she wrote them in order of their importance. She began with the reason most important to her.

Working It Out

Here's the map from Lesson 35. It's the plan for a paragraph to persuade people not to drive when drunk.

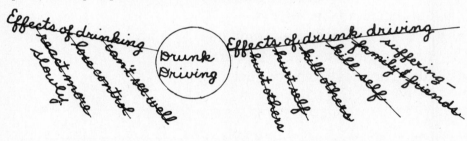

The main idea for the paragraph is not to drive when drunk. Write a topic sentence for the paragraph.

_____

The writer started to write his paragraph. It is printed at the top of the next page. He wrote about the effects of drinking. Finish the paragraph for him. Use the details from the map in the sentences you write. Write about the effects of drunk driving. Put the most important effect first.

■ When you drink too much, you lose control of your body. You do not see as well. You react much more slowly. For these reasons, you simply cannot drive as well as usual. If you try to drive while drunk, you can cause some horrible things to happen.

_____

_____

_____

_____

✏️ _Writing On Your Own_

Look back at the outline or map you made for Writing on Your Own in Lesson 35. It gives ideas you can use to persuade someone to hire you.

Put the main idea of your map or outline in a sentence. This will be the topic sentence of your persuasive paragraph.

_____

Next, use the details from your map or outline to write the other sentences in your paragraph. Put the details in order of importance. Write the ideas _you_ think are most important first. Copy your topic sentence. Then write the rest of your first draft. Remember that your first draft does not have to be perfect.

_____

_____

_____

_____

▲ Looking Back

For the first draft of a persuasive paragraph, put your main idea in a good topic sentence. Then use your details to write the other sentences. Put the details in an order that makes your ideas clear and persuasive.

Revising and Editing a Persuasive Paragraph

> *In this lesson you will*
> - revise a persuasive paragraph
> - edit a persuasive paragraph

Getting Started

You've prewritten and written the first draft of a persuasive paragraph. In this lesson you know you'll revise and edit the paragraph.

Here's the first draft of one paragraph. It tries to persuade someone to learn to swim.

- If you see a person drownding, you can save him. You would be a hero swiming is good exercise too. It help you feel good and take off some weight. If you ever fall into deep water, you can save yourself. It is fun too. You will have a good time at the beach or in a pool if you can swim. So therefore lern to swim. You'll be happy if you do.

Do you see that the paragraph has no topic sentence? The writer has some problem sentences too. Some run on. Others are short and choppy. One detail seems out of order.

The writer knew a first draft is never perfect. She revised and then edited her paragraph.

Here's an Example

Here is how the writer revised and edited her paragraph. Read it carefully to see the kinds of changes she made. The writer used the checklists in the margin. If you don't remember the exact questions, review the long checklists on pages 187–188.

review the long checklists on pages 187–188.

Do yourself a big favor — learn to swim.

If you see a person drowning, you can save him. You would be a hero. *Swimming* swimming is ~~good~~ *also excellent* exercise ~~too~~. It help*s* you feel good and take off some weight. If you ever fall into deep water, you can save yourself. It is fun too. You will have ~~a good~~ *an enjoyable* time at the beach or in a pool if you can swim. ~~So~~ /therefore, ~~lern~~ *learn* to swim. You'll be happy if you do.

The woman wrote a strong command for her topic sentence. She moved a sentence to keep her details in order of importance. She revised short, choppy sentences, and then she edited a run on. She edited mistakes in grammar and spelling too.

The writer revised and edited her first draft into a good persuasive paragraph.

Working It Out

Below is the first draft of a letter. A father is writing to his son. He's trying to persuade the son to come home and join the family business. Revise the letter. Read it several times if necessary to improve it as best you can. Then edit it. Use the short checklists on this page or the long checklists on pages 187–188 if you need to.

■ You should come to work with us in the family bakery. You could make a living here. You'll earn good money and get raises in the futur. Someday you will become your own boss. Also, you'll be helping bild our family's name in the neighborhood. Carrying on a family

tradition. It would make your mother and me feel good,

think about coming to work with us.

✐ *Writing On Your Own*

Go back to the paragraph you wrote in Writing on Your Own in
Lesson 36. It persuades someone to give you a job. Revise the
paragraph carefully. Read and revise it several times if you need
to. Then edit it. Use the short checklists on page 226 or the long
checklists on pages 187–188 if you must. Finally, rewrite your
paragraph here.

_____

_____

_____

_____

_____

_____

_____

_____

▲ Looking Back

After you write the first draft of a persuasive paragraph, be sure
to revise it. Then edit it for mistakes. If you follow these steps,
you'll produce a good paragraph. You may even persuade your
reader!

When You Need More Than One Paragraph

In this lesson you will
- write more than one paragraph to tell your message

Getting Started

Often one paragraph is enough for all you want to say. But other times you need to write more. You can't fit your message into one paragraph.

In a paragraph, you state the main idea in a topic sentence. Then you write several sentences to explain the main idea.

In a longer piece of writing, you state the main idea of the whole piece. Then you write several paragraphs to explain it. You can tell much more in several paragraphs than you can in several sentences.

Here's an Example

A manager needed to write a memo about three rules. He wrote his topic sentence. Then he stated the three rules. They are the details that support his main idea. His last sentence ends his message.

- All workers must follow these rules. You must sign the "Sign In" sheet when you come to work. All workers must wear plastic gloves when they work with food. Every worker must wear a company hat. Thank you for following these rules.

The manager read his memo. He decided he needed to tell more. Each detail should be explained to the workers. So the manager wrote this longer memo about the rules.

■ All workers must follow these rules. They are important. Please read them carefully.

You must sign the "Sign In" sheet when you come to work. The sheet is on the desk in my office. Please sign your name and the time you come in. If you do not sign the sheet, you will not get paid.

All workers must wear plastic gloves when they work with food. This is a state law. We must follow it. It is to keep germs from getting into the food.

Every worker must wear a company hat. The hat will keep your hair out of the food. This rule also is a state law. Hats may be picked up in my office.

Thank you for following these rules.

The manager stated his main idea in the first short paragraph. Then he wrote one paragraph about each rule. Each paragraph begins with its own main idea. These main ideas had been the supporting details in his first memo. Now the workers will understand *why* the rules are important.

Working It Out

Suppose you're writing a letter to a friend about your favorite holidays. Your topic sentence is "I have two favorite holidays." In a paragraph, you could name the two days and tell one or two reasons that you like each. Fill in the blanks in these sentences. They could be the supporting details about the two holidays in the paragraph.

I like _____ because _____ .

I also like _____ because _____ .

Suppose you want to tell *more* about each holiday. You'd have to write a paragraph about each one. In each paragraph, you'd explain the things you like about that day.

Write the names of your two favorite holidays. Then list more details about each one.

Holiday 1 _____   **Holiday 2** _____

_____   _____

_____   _____

_____   _____

✏️ ⟹ *Writing On Your Own*

Finish the letter to a friend about favorite holidays. First, write the topic sentence "I have two favorite holidays." Make a short lead-in paragraph for your letter. Add one or two sentences to that topic sentence.

_____

_____

Use your list of ideas as you would an outline. Write a paragraph about holiday 1. Start with the topic sentence "I like _____ because _____ ." Then use the details you listed to write the other sentences.

_____

_____

_____

_____

Write a paragraph about holiday 2. Start with the topic sentence "I also like _____ because _____ ." Use the details you listed to write the other sentences.

_____

_____

_____

_____

Write a very short paragraph to sum up your letter. One or two sentences will be enough.

_____

_____

Don't forget to revise and then edit your letter.

▲ Looking Back

Sometimes you need more than one paragraph to tell your message. You write your main idea in the first short paragraph. You explain each supporting detail in its own paragraph. Then you write a short closing paragraph.

Essay Writing

> *In this lesson you will*
> ■ get ready to write an essay

Picture It

You now know how to write a paragraph. If you can write a paragraph, writing an essay is not hard. An essay is a group of related paragraphs explaining one main idea. Look at this chart. You can see how an essay is organized like a paragraph.

	Paragraph	**Essay**
Opening	topic sentence that tells main idea of paragraph	short paragraph of 2–3 sentences that tell main idea of whole essay
Body	sentences telling about main idea (each sentence is a supporting detail)	paragraphs telling about main idea (each paragraph explains a supporting detail)
Ending	sentence that sums up	short paragraph that sums up

Here's an Example

A student wrote this paragraph. His topic was why people choose to marry.

- Men and women marry for different reasons. Most people get married because they love the other person. Some people marry so they will have a companion, a person to share time, thoughts, and feelings with them. Other people get married for practical reasons such as saving money. Marriage helps people fill these needs.

This paragraph could be made into an essay. Each sentence could be the topic sentence of a paragraph. Each paragraph could explain the idea given in the sentence. The writer could make a plan like this to turn his paragraph into an essay.

Main idea: Men and women marry for different reasons.

1. Most people get married because they love the other person.
   need to care and be cared for
   marriage vow brings secure feeling
   gives contentment and happiness

2. Some people marry so they will have a companion, a person to share time, thoughts, and feelings with them.
   does away with loneliness
   go places together
   share good and bad times

3. Other people get married for practical reasons, like saving money.
   two to share the rent, food expenses, etc.
   share work

The writer could add facts, examples, and reasons to explain the details given in each paragraph. He would write a whole paragraph about each reason. He would also write a short opening and ending paragraph.

Working It Out

The writer in Here's an Example wrote a paragraph about why people get married. Then he made an outline for an essay on the same topic. Now it's your turn to use your own paragraph to plan an essay.

Take this topic: Why are fast-food restaurants popular?
Write a paragraph on the reasons.

_____

_____

_____

_____

_____

_____

Writing On Your Own

Use the paragraph you just wrote about fast-food restaurants.
Make an outline for an essay on the same topic. Fill in details
under the ideas from the paragraph sentences. Use the outline
in Here's an Example as a model.

▲ Looking Back

Writing an essay is like writing a paragraph. You think of ideas
about a topic, and discover a main idea. In an essay, however,
each detail becomes the main idea of its own paragraph.

Whenever you write, remember to prewrite, write a first draft,
revise, edit, and then write your final copy. You want everything
you write to show you at your best!

Measuring What You've Learned

You've finished all the lessons in this book. It's time to see how much your writing skills have improved.

This section asks you to go through the whole writing process. You will do prewriting, writing the first draft, revising, editing, and presenting your final paragraph. These are all the steps you've learned in this book.

Read the directions carefully as you do this section.

Directions: Write a paragraph on **one** of the following topics. The paragraph should be 8 to 10 sentences long.

- one thing everyone should learn to do
- people who are important to you
- the importance of relaxing
- the good things about this country

Choose one topic from the list above. Circle the topic. Then follow all these steps to write your paragraph.

Step 1: Getting ideas to write about
Brainstorm. In the space below, jot down all the ideas you can about the topic. OR ask yourself these questions about the topic: *Who? What? When? Where? Why? How?* OR use both ways to get ideas.

Step 2: Finding the main idea
Look at all the ideas you wrote down. What main idea comes to your mind? Write it on the line below.

Step 3: Selecting details

Check each idea you wrote in Step 1 that could be used to tell about your main idea. Add details if you think of them.

Step 4: Organizing your ideas

Use the main idea and details to make an outline or a map. The outline or map should help you organize your ideas for the paragraph.

Step 5: Writing the topic sentence

Look at the main idea you've chosen. State that idea in a complete sentence on the line below. This will be the topic sentence of your paragraph.

_____

Step 6: Writing the first draft

Write your topic sentence on the first line below. Now use the supporting details to write the other sentences in your paragraph.

_____
_____
_____
_____
_____
_____
_____
_____

Step 7: Revising your paragraph

Now read your first draft to see how you can improve it. Read it several times to focus on each of these things: your main idea, supporting details, explanations of details, order, missing ideas, linking words, sentence variety, and specific, concise wording. Mark your changes between the lines.

Step 8: Editing your paragraph

Check your writing for mistakes in capitalization, punctuation, spelling, and grammar. Write your corrections between the lines.

Step 9: Writing the final copy

You've followed all the steps in the writing process but one. On the lines below, write the final copy of your paragraph. Try to make it the best paragraph you can write.

_____

_____

_____

_____

_____

_____

_____

_____

_____

Your Results

Now that you've finished your paragraph, ask your teacher to score it for you.

If you did well on this section, congratulations! You have learned a lot. You're ready to go on to study GED writing.

If you had some problems, you need to go back and review some of the lessons in this book. Your teacher will show you which ones. After you review, try Measuring What You've Learned again.

Part A
Answers

Measuring What You Know
pages 2–4

There are (1) several ways to be a good cook. For example, some people refuse to follow a (2) recipe. They like to (3) guess at what to add next. These cooks are interesting because they never (4) repeat a meal!

5. Barry has some strange ideas.

6. We went to Maryville last weekend.

7. The girls want bicycles for Christmas.

8. I am tired of cleaning all the time.

9. You were wrong about Rick.

10. Tony went to the gym for a workout.

11. The Carsons walked a mile to the store.

12. I did pushups twice a day.

Possible sentences:

13. The summer storm passed swiftly over the quiet town.

14. Jackie read for hours in the silent, dusty library.

Note: For questions 13 and 14, many other sentences are possible. Ask your teacher to check your sentences.

15. One never knows if one will win or lose.
or
You never know if you will win or lose.

16. Each kitten has a white spot on its nose.

17. Judge Ramirez told Raymond to tell the truth.

18. It's easy to learn how to drive.

19. Stephanie will choose a new partner in September.

20. This stew has too much garlic in it.

21. The Grabowskis are putting a pool in their yard.

22. During summer, I swim every Thursday.

Possible sentences:

23. We were glad to relax after a long day.

24. The baby monkey, quick and alert, climbed up the tree.

25. Egg rolls are served in many Chinese restaurants.

26. What kind of varnish should I use on this desk?

Note: For numbers 23–26, your sentences will be different. Have your teacher check them to see if they are correct.

Possible sentences:

27. One cold, rainy day Marcia felt sad.

28. We went with Casey to a movie last night.

29. Jeff sang like a rock-and-roll star at the concert.

30. Dolphins swim quickly and very gracefully.

31. Darlene and Dave like to travel.

32. Mike works during the day and studies at night.

33. The player slid into home, but the umpire called an out.

34. After we shopped for groceries, we made dinner.

35. The wash had dried, so I took it off the line.

36. Since Hans will finish on Thursday, he won't work on Friday.

Note: Other sentence combinations are possible for questions 27–36. If your sentences are different from these, ask your teacher to see if they are correct.

37. Possible summary: Today's secretaries use computers, work for a group of people, and have many new jobs to do.

Part A / Lesson 1

Picture It
page 8

Sample answer:
Mother: What do you think you're doing?
Son: Oh, hi, Mom. Want a cookie?

Working It Out
page 9

1. *b*

2. *b*

3. *a*

2. List of groceries:
For whom? Antonio
Why? to help him remember what to buy.

3. TV Repair invoice:
For whom? Jim O'Connor
Why? to tell him how much to pay for the repairs

4. letter:
For whom? Lupe
Why? to find out if she is coming to visit.

Writing On Your Own
page 10

Sample answer:
Patient's Name: *Martha Collins*
Date: *February 7, 1990*
Symptoms: I started feeling sick on *Tuesday.* At first my throat felt *sore* and I had a fever. After a day, I began *to feel dizzy* and that was when I decided to see a doctor. Right now I feel *weak* and my throat *is still sore.*

Part A / **Lesson 2**

Here's an Example
pages 11–12

1. Topic: Donna's bad cold

2. Topic: Frank's job

3. Topic: Eddie's garden

Working It Out
pages 12–13

1. The topic is *a drawbridge.* The paragraph describes how the drawbridge is raised and lowered.

2. The topic is *not clear.*

3. The topic is *violence on TV.* The paragraph describes how parents worry when their children see violence on television.

4. The topic is *not clear.*

Writing On Your Own
page 13

Sample answers:
Susan: Lisa is late again, Bill. I told her to be home by 5:30.
Bill: Did you call the school? Maybe she *is still there.*

Susan: I called, but there's no answer. I'm really worried.
Bill: Did you call Tisha's mother? Maybe Lisa and Tisha *went over to Tisha's house.*
Susan: Their line is busy.
Bill: Did you drive past the video arcade? Maybe she *stopped there on the way home.*
Susan: She'd better not have. I've told her over and over that *she should not go there without asking us first.*
The topic of this conversation is *where Lisa might be.*

Sample sentences:
My children love to go to parades. They like to watch the marching bands and listen to the music.

Part A / **Lesson 3**

After you have completed this lesson, show your work to your teacher or a friend. Ask if your handwriting is easy to read. Ask which letters, numbers, or words are difficult to read. Practice writing these letters, numbers, and words in your journal.

Part A / **Lesson 4**

Here's an Example
page 19

Sample answers:
dancing: music, twirl
mirror: reflection, seeing
forgotten: past, lost
taxes: money, high

Working It Out
pages 19–20

There is no "right" answer for this. Answers will vary.

Writing On Your Own
page 20

Sample answer:
Today is Thursday, the time is 11:30 A.M., and I am sitting here at my desk writing in this book and thinking about having lunch soon. I hope there will still be hot dogs in the cafeteria. Sometimes they run out early. I like hot dogs with ketchup and mustard. I don't really like hamburgers but I do like pizza. Sometimes I **Stop!**

Part A / **Lesson 5**

Picture It
page 21

1. c. *Biltrons* could be *tools,* since Mildred is complaining that Hubert left them on something (the *creeblop*). You couldn't leave *anger* or *cold* anywhere.

2. a. *Creeblop* could be *floor* since something (the *biltrons*) was left *on* it. You couldn't leave anything on *summer* or *peace.*

3. c. Hubert tells Mildred she treats the Newtrons like *gondrords* instead of next-door neighbors. It makes sense to say that Mildred treats the Newtrons like *movie stars.* It doesn't make sense to say she treats them like *popcorn* or *happy.*

Here's an Example
page 22

1. c. If the baby *eats all the time,* then *appetite* must mean *hunger.*

2. c. If the garden has lots of cucumbers, carrots, and tomatoes, then *flourishing* must mean *growing well.*

3. a. If the band played only the first two verses of the song, to say they *omitted* the third verse must mean they *left it out.*

4. a. If the hero died at the end of the movie, a *tragedy* must mean a *sad story.*

Working It Out
pages 22–23

Karen opened the door of her apartment. She was <u>shocked.</u>
₁
"What happened?" she gasped, <u>walking</u> into her living
₂
room. <u>Chairs</u> and lamps were
₃
tipped over. Her sofa pillows were <u>ripped.</u> Her
₄
books were thrown all over the <u>floor.</u> Karen stared <u>at</u> the
₅ ₆
table where her television set usually stood. The <u>television</u>
₇
was gone. "I've been <u>robbed!</u>"
₈
she screamed.

1a. Doctors are afraid Peggy's brain was *damaged* in the accident.

1b. When Cindy left him, Ralph's heart was *broken.*

2a. Tom's carelessness almost *cost* him his life.

2b. The sale *price* of this dress is twenty dollars.

3a. My children always *argue* about sharing toys.

3b. The *debate* between the candidates for mayor is at 8 P.M.

4a. Raul *tells* his children a story before they go to bed.

4b. Lillian *says* she'll be home tonight.

Writing On Your Own
page 23

Sample answers:

1. We frequently go camping in the Blair Woods on weekends.

2. Grandma hasn't had a big appetite since she was sick.

3. After two days of rain, the corn crop is flourishing.

4. The president omitted part of her speech.

5. The plane crash was a great tragedy.

Part A / **Lesson 6**

Working It Out
page 26

1. freedom, frog. You can find them at the top of the page.

2. (Friday) from (frequent) (friend)

3. (freedem) freeze friction

4. freeway

5. French

6. c. These are all tools you might use in doing home repairs.

7. d. These words are all related to health and first aid.

8. a. All these words have to do with cooking.

9. b. All these words are parts of a car.

Writing On Your Own
page 27

Words, definitions, and sentences will vary.

Part A / **Lesson 7**

Working It Out
pages 29–30

Sample answers:
Housecleaning: bucket, sponge, paper towel, sweeping, mopping, vacuum cleaner, furniture, floors, carpet
Taking the Bus: ticket, crowded, getting on, getting off, transfer, talking, reading, paying, sleeping

Writing On Your Own
page 30

Sample word list:
Vacation: relaxing, beach, towels, swimming suit, waves, sand, ice cream, radio, mosquitoes, eating, jogging, sleeping, blanket, picnic

Sample word map: See Fig. A.

Figure A: Word map for Part A, Lesson 7, page 30

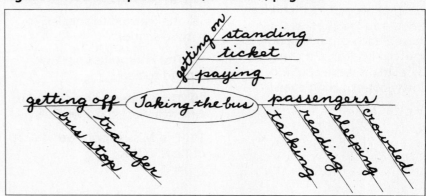

Part A / **Lesson 8**

Working It Out
page 32

Sample answers:

2. The angry old bear chased the yelping dogs.

3. The clever spy quietly left the airport on foot.

4. The blazing sun rose swiftly over the pale mountains.

Describing your chair
Sample answers:
brown, squeaky, hard, wood

Describing your closet
Sample answers:
full, dusty, old clothes, broken toys, stale air, dark, quiet, small

Writing On Your Own
page 33

Describing an outdoor party

Sample answers:
Seeing: old picnic table, friends, orange sunset
Hearing: laughter, children yelling, rock music
Smelling: pine trees, flowers, fresh coffee
Tasting: cold soda, crispy potato chips, marshmallows
Touching: soft grass, cool breeze, scratchy bushes

Sample sentences:
My friends and I stood around the old picnic table, enjoying the cool breeze. Our children yelled and laughed as they chased each other through the scratchy bushes. On the grill, juicy steaks were cooking slowly over sizzling coals.

Part A / **Lesson 9**

Getting Started
page 34

Sample answers:
I think the world would be a better place without: earthquakes, traffic jams, hatred, cigarettes, war, money, broccoli
The nouns you should underline are shown below.

poverty	sunshine
arrange	quickly
marriage	bury
Maple Street	great

Lake Tahoe	kitchen
pour	disappear
Conrad Braun	career
jealous	happiness

Here's an Example
pages 35–36

2. Franklin Roosevelt was president during the Great Depression.

3. My friend Paula used to work for Amoco. *(OK)*

4. Grace Kelly became a princess when she married Prince Rainier.

5. Nathan Bradley would like to become mayor.

6. We invited Dr. Ortiz, Mayor Todd, and the president. *(OK)*

7. My family celebrates all the Jewish holidays.

8. She learned to speak German in school.

9. The Philippines once belonged to Spain.

10. The Chinese who settled in America were hard workers.

11. The Mississippi River is east of here. *(OK)*

12. Many oil tankers cross the Atlantic Ocean.

13. Newark is in the East. *(OK)*

14. The Midwest has miles and miles of good farmland. *(OK)*

15. The Millers live near Central Park in New York.

16. The building on the corner is two hundred years old.

17. The Westons live on Munster Avenue.

18. During the winter, I usually gain weight.

19. Even though it's October, it still seems like summer. *(OK)*

Working It Out
page 36

Last summer Greg went to California to visit his grandmother. She lives in Oakland, which is east of San Francisco. One day Greg and his grandmother drove across the Golden Gate Bridge. After hearing about it for many years, Greg was happy to finally see the world-famous bridge.

Writing On Your Own
page 37

Sample answers:
My full name is Walter Perez. (Rule 1)
The date of my birth is August 8, 1967. (Rule 6)
The place I was born is called Pensacola, Florida. (Rule 5)
The three states I would most like to visit are New York, Colorado, and Kansas. (Rule 5)

My favorite city is <u>San Antonio,</u>
<u>Texas</u>. (Rule 5)
My favorite season of the year
is <u>summer</u>. (Rule 6)
My favorite musician is <u>Willie</u>
<u>Nelson</u>. (Rule 1)
If I were in politics, I would like
to be elected as <u>county judge</u>.
(Rule 2)

Part A / **Lesson 10**

Working It Out
page 40

2. Jay will ask Sue for a date.
<u>He</u> will ask <u>her</u> out tomorrow.

3. We have a son.
Our son wants a bicycle for <u>his</u>
birthday.

4. Lisa has new glasses.
<u>She</u> bought <u>them</u> two weeks
ago.

5. You gave a sock to the dog.
<u>Your</u> sock is in <u>its</u> mouth.

Sample answers:

7. Someone left <u>her</u> dress on
the floor.

8. Jack called Ed yesterday. <u>Ed</u>
has a cold.

9. My neighbors have cats. I
don't let <u>their cats</u> in my
house.

10. That car has <u>its</u> headlights
on.

Writing On Your Own
page 41

Sample answer:
Credit cards are popular in the
United States. Many people
use them often. Be careful,
however, when you buy something with a credit card. Unless
you pay for it quickly, you are
charged a high rate of interest.
A credit card can be helpful,
but it can also be expensive.

Part A / **Lesson 11**

Picture It
pages 42–43

Sample sentences:
A <u>monkey</u> rides two horses.
A bear on roller skates <u>chases</u>
<u>after them</u>.

1. *a*
2. *c*
3. *b*
4. *d*

Here's an Example
page 43

I think
you think
he
she ⟩ thinks
it
we think
they think
I reach
you reach
he
she ⟩ reaches
it
we reach
they reach

Working It Out
page 44

1. You <u>do</u> not know me, and
he <u>does</u> know me.

2. He <u>likes</u> Debbie a lot, and
we <u>like</u> her too.

3. I <u>agree</u> with Marvin and he
<u>agrees</u> with me.

         She
2. ~~Bridget~~ (<u>wants</u>/want) to
vacation in Mexico this winter.

        They
3. ~~The neighbors~~ (goes/<u>go</u>)
out of town every weekend.

Writing On Your Own
page 45

2. Donald <u>has</u> a terrible cold.

3. The horses <u>are</u> in the
meadow.

4. We <u>have</u> three small
children.

■ At three A.M., Bruno Ponti
<u>parks</u> his ambulance outside
Diana's home. "We <u>have</u> to
hurry!" say her frightened parents. The ambulance <u>speeds</u>
toward the hospital. Minutes
later, doctors and nurses <u>are</u>
working to save Diana's life.

Part A / **Lesson 12**

Here's an Example
pages 47–48

[1] present event
Sergio <u>cleans</u> his apartment
now.
or
Sergio <u>is cleaning</u> his apartment now.
[2] future event
Sergio <u>will clean</u> his apartment
next week.
[3] past event
Sergio <u>cleaned</u> his apartment
yesterday.
[4] past and continuing event
Sergio <u>has cleaned</u> his apartment many times.
[5] past event before another
past event
Sergio <u>had cleaned</u> his apartment before he went out.

1. *Years ago Margaret <u>danced</u>*
whenever she could. The
phrase *years ago* tells you that
the verb time should be in the
past.

2. *Next month the class will study nutrition.* The phrase *next month* tells you that the verb time should be in the **future.**

3. *Before she moved away from home, Leticia had started saving money.* The phrase *before she moved* tells you that the verb time should describe a **past event before another past event.**

4. *For many years the Schmidts have loved to travel.* The phrase *for many years* tells you the verb time should describe a **past and continuing event.**

5. *Every time Donald speaks he bores everyone.* The phrase *every time* tells you that the verb time should be in the **present.**

Working It Out
pages 48–49

1. saw
2. have eaten, or ate
3. correct
4. have done or did
5. takes
6. had begun
7. will have
8. correct

1. The band will try to keep the crowd happy.

2. The ranger will see many unusual birds in the forest.

3. Peter will study all week for the exam.

Writing On Your Own
page 49

One week ago the Farmers' Trust Bank announced it

is buying the Jasper farm on Rte. 17. "We have been working on this farm for seventy years," said Joe Jasper. "Now we have seen our land sold to someone else."

It is unclear if the Jaspers will move. Last week bank president Albert Givson said, "We need someone to grow crops on that land. Maybe the Jaspers will want to stay."

Part A / **Lesson 13**

Working It Out
pages 51–52

Sample answers:

2. Chef Raoul will prepare the dessert.

3. The marchers carried the banners.

4. Our neighbors always watch us.

5. Toni Johnson sings "Another Love."

Sample answers:

2. "I can't find my wallet," Art gasps.

3. The birds stole all the seeds I planted.

4. Corey crawled into the tunnel.

5. Andre will borrow some money.

Writing On Your Own
page 52

Sample answer:
■ We entered a cafe and ordered coffee. The men in black raincoats slipped in after us. They were still watching us. Their presence frightened us. Suddenly one of them asked, "Aren't you the Prince and

Princess of Liechtenstein?" "Certainly not!" I laughed. "Well, what a waste of time!" he snapped, and the two men quickly left the cafe.

Part A / **Lesson 14**

Working It Out
pages 55–56

■ When you have a job interview, remember these suggestions. First of all, dress neatly. Don't wear blue jeans or tennis shoes. Second, don't chew gum or smoke. Third, find out about the company ahead of time. Write down some questions to ask during the interview to show your interest in the business. Finally, after the interview, write a short note or call the company to thank the people for spending time with you. Mention again how much you'd like to work for the company.
■ Every four years, the people of the United States elect a president. The two major political parties, the Democrats and the Republicans, each pick a candidate. These candidates are chosen at a national convention a few months before the election. Although there are always candidates from other, smaller political parties, it would be quite surprising if someone other than a Democrat or a Republican became president.

Writing On Your Own
page 56

Sample answers:

2. The choir is singing at the Christmas concert.

3. The cat, damp and shivering, waited outside the door.

4. Since Carla was frightened, Nancy walked her home.

5. Arnold said the party was Friday.

Sample sentences:
I think that women should be allowed to run for president. Women pay taxes like everybody else. They should have the same rights as everybody else. I think a woman would make a good president.

Part A / **Lesson 15**

Working It Out
pages 58–59

Sample answers:

2. There is a doctor on the plane.

3. Why can't we go swimming?

4. The Tanakas have three children.

5. Where are the eggs?

Sample answers:

2. Turn left at the next light.

3. Save more money.

4. Bring me the newspaper.

Writing On Your Own
page 59

Sample answers:

1. The robbers ran out of the bank.

2. How much money did they steal?

3. Stop those robbers!

4. I can't believe they robbed the bank!

Part A / **Lesson 16**

Here's an Example
page 61

1. After Leslie saw the doctor, she felt better.

2. Leslie saw the doctor.

Working It Out
pages 61–62

1. S

2. F; the *verb* is missing.

3. S

4. S

5. F; the *verb* is missing.

6. S

7. F; the *subject* is missing.

8. F; the *complete thought* is missing.

9. S

10. F; the *complete thought* is missing.

Sample answers:

2. The old house was full of bats and spiders.

3. Whenever Jim and Felicia call us back, we're not home.

4. Rachel talked in her sleep.

5. John crossed the street without noticing the traffic light.

6. From the moment we walked in the door, we wanted to leave.

7. Since Susan and Greg are going, I will too.

8. Jack felt happy.

Writing On Your Own
page 62

Sample paragraph:
Do you know how to relax? Walking is a good way to get away from your problems. Walking can give you time to think things through.

Part A / **Lesson 17**

Working It Out
pages 64–65

2. correct

3. comma splice

4. correct

5. run-on

Writing On Your Own
page 65

Sample answers:

1. Luisa woke up late. She was late for work.

2. The winners were announced, and Abdul won fifty dollars.

3. Gas rates are high; some families can't afford heat.

4. The cat jumped. He landed on the table.

5. We screamed; we were very scared.

Sample paragraph:
If you are a smoker, you have probably noticed more and more "No Smoking" signs. In some cities strict laws have been passed. They forbid smoking in restaurants and offices. Fewer people smoke today since everyone knows about the risk of cancer. Maybe someday cigarettes will be a thing of the past.

Part A / Lesson 18

Working It Out
pages 67–68

1. The lively, graceful dancers leaped around the stage.

2. The angry old woman demanded a refund.

3. The police team worked slowly, carefully, and skillfully to take apart the bomb.

4. The tired and hungry child cried herself to sleep.

5. My car broke down on a cold, windy, and snowy evening.

Sample sentences:

2. Cara's shiny red car was parked in the driveway.

3. My new job is difficult but exciting.

4. Laddie ran out the door, down the path, and into the woods.

Writing On Your Own
page 68

Sample answers:
Camping scene—cooking supper, wet, unhappy
Traffic scene—directing traffic, hot, sweaty

Sample sentences:

2. The wet, unhappy campers had to cook supper in a pouring rain.

3. Pete was hot and sweaty as he directed traffic.

Part A / Lesson 19

Working It Out
pages 70–71

Sample answers:

2. On Friday, Rafael will take the GED exam at Dane College.

3. The Gardners are angry at the Webers.

4. Because of a flat tire, the bus will be late this afternoon.

Sample answers:

1. After the concert, Phyllis and David argued about their marriage.

2. Luis quit smoking five years ago after his heart attack.

3. The Gorskis shop every Saturday at Carter Super Foods.

Writing On Your Own
page 71

Sample answers:

1. Last summer, the famous actress robbed a bank as a joke.

2. My son Robert once hiked twenty miles to stay out of trouble.

3. After a lot of thought, I will leave the company next month.

4. The Arnauds want to adopt a child next month for the wrong reason.

5. I once robbed a bank to help a friend.

Part A / Lesson 20

Getting Started
page 72

Attention Mrs. Rosalie Steele! You and your husband each have six chances to win our Luxury Sweepstakes. You could win one of our grand prizes. You might drive home in a new car, or fly to Florida for a seven-day vacation, or take a cruise to the Bahamas.
To enter our Luxury Sweepstakes, fill out the enclosed entry blank. Sign and return it by midnight on April 1st.

Here's an Example
pages 73–74

Sample answers:

1. Petra and Jean like to bowl.

2. My dog, cat, and goldfish are hungry.

3. Either Ralph or Judy will be fired.

4. Neither Paco nor Richard came over.

5. Roman fixes cars and builds engines.

6. My aunt either watches TV or plays cards.

Working It Out
pages 74–75

2. Either Anne or Beth danced with Kevin.

3. Neither Leroy nor the Grants sing.

4. The dog wagged her tail and barked at me.

5. Mark or Jay could have come earlier.

6. Tony either called his mother or went to see her.

7. Mrs. Johnson left her house and walked to the car.

8. Jane or the children are tired.

9. I drove a truck and operated a crane.

10. We'll either have a party or go to the shore.

11. The baby does not walk or talk.

12. The bus and the train go there.

13. Neither the bank nor the post office was open.

Writing On Your Own
page 75

Sample paragraph:
People have different opinions about hair. Movie stars and teenagers spend lots of money to find the right hairstyle. However, some people don't worry about hair. They may keep it very short, let it grow out long, or even shave it off completely.

Part A / **Lesson 21**

Working It Out
pages 77–78

Sample answers:

1. Jon is coming over, <u>and</u> he's bringing Janet.

2. Mary wants to come, <u>but</u> she might have to work.

3. Willie gets off at ten, <u>so</u> he'll be a little late.

4. Eva had better hurry, <u>or</u> she won't make it on time.

5. Everyone will bring something, <u>so</u> we don't have to cook.

Sample answers:

2. Lisa is on another diet, but she still eats ice cream sundaes.

3. Amy will borrow money, or she'll have to go home.

4. Hector changed jobs last month, and now his wife has a new job.

5. Dogs are smart animals, but pigs are even smarter.

Writing On Your Own
page 78

Sample answers:

2. The weather report promised sunny skies for Saturday, <u>but instead it rained.</u>

3. Senator Dawson barely won the last election<u>, and he may lose this one.</u>

4. Smoke was pouring out from under the hood of the car<u>, so Bill pulled over.</u>

5. Cathy has had problems with her boss, <u>yet she doesn't want to quit.</u>

Part A / **Lesson 22**

Picture It
page 79

While Annette <u>was balancing a tray of drinks</u>, Louise <u>stood up suddenly.</u>

Here's an Example
pages 80–81

1. If you want to stay, we can stay.

2. We can stay if you want to stay.

Sample sentences:

1. Unless you have a good reason, I won't let you leave early.

2. Even though you have a good reason, I won't let you leave early.

Working It Out
pages 81–82

Sample answers:

2. Although Cynthia is tired, she'll work late.

3. Once Shelley calls about the movie, we'll decide if we're going.

4. Jan will finish the project since Ahmed doesn't have time.

5. After the rain stopped, the sun came out.

6. Sally can afford a vacation because she got her tax refund.

Writing On Your Own
page 82

Sample answers:

2. Barry drove home slowly after he saw the accident.

3. Even though we were scared, we watched the movie.

4. This trail will be easier to follow once we leave the woods.

5. After Maria's visit, Ellen was happy.

6. Chris will get a new job if she passes this test.

7. When Mary won the lottery, she bought a house.

8. I asked him to look at my car because it made a strange noise.

9. My wife always gets mad when I leave the bathroom dirty.

10. Just as Mr. Ramos pulled into his driveway, the rain started.

Part A / **Lesson 23**

Here's an Example
page 84

You should have written phrases like these:
Line 5: next summer
Line 6: cut down on traffic jams

Figure B: Notes for Part A, Lesson 23, page 86

Line 7: Harter Heights and Greenview
Line 9: against new freeway

Working It Out
page 85

You should have written phrases like these:
Line 2: —more people would go to malls
      —local businesses lose customers
Line 3: Fremont has character—life moves slower
      —shouldn't tear down homes to move faster
Conclusion: Fremont doesn't need another freeway

Writing On Your Own
page 86

Sample notes: See Fig. B.

Part A / Lesson 24

Picture It
page 87

Refrigerator: milk, eggs
Freezer: ice cream, juice
Kitchen Cupboard: cereal, soup
Bathroom Closet: bath soap, shampoo

Here's an Example
page 88

My Daily Routine
  I. Morning
    A. Get kids to school
      1. Make breakfast
      2. Walk kids to bus stop
    B. Get to work by 9 A.M.
  II. Afternoon
    A. Stop at store
    B. Pick up kids at baby-sitter
 III. Evening
    A. Fix supper
    B. Get kids to bed
    C. Clean house
      1. Do laundry
      2. Take out trash

Working It Out
page 89

Sample outline:
Test-Taking Tips
  I. Before the test
    A. Study
      1. Take notes on important points
      2. Make up questions and try to answer them
      3. Study a little at a time
    B. Relax after you study
      1. Exercise or stretch
      2. Think positive

Writing On Your Own
page 90

Sample outline:
  II. During the test

    A. Have everything you need close by
      1. Bring extra pencils and pens
      2. Keep answer sheet next to test
    B. Keep track of time
      1. Do the questions you know first
      2. Go back and do the hard ones
    C. Check your work
      1. Go over all your answers
      2. Make sure the answers match the questions
      3. Answer questions you skipped
      4. Use all the time you have

Part A / Lesson 25

Working It Out
pages 92–93

1. B, *She spoke in a loud voice*, should be crossed out. This detail is not needed in a summary.

2. because it is not very important

3. Sample summary: Before the Civil War, Sojourner traveled all over the North preaching against slavery.

4. Paragraph B is the best summary because it repeats all the most important details. Paragaph A is not a good summary. It doesn't give the main point of Sojourner's speech—that women can be strong. It also gives some unimportant details. Paragraph C is not a good summary, either. Like Paragraph A, it does not give the main point of Sojourner's speech. It also sounds as though Sojourner went to the convention right after winning

her son's freedom. But the convention was many years later. Finally, it says her words against *racism* are still remembered. Her words at the convention were against *sexism,* not racism. Her fight against *both* racism and sexism is still remembered today.

Writing On Your Own
page 93

1. Sample summary: Before you take a test, you should study and relax. When you study, take notes and go over them. Ask yourself questions. Study a little every day. After you study, relax by stretching or exercising, and think positive. When you take the test, have everything you need close by. Keep track of time, and be sure to check your work very carefully.

Part A / Lesson 26

Getting Started
page 94

1. accept. The words *accept* and *except* have been confused. *I can't accept what you're saying* is the correct sentence.

2. They're. The possessive pronoun *their* has been confused with the contraction *they're. They're going to the beach tomorrow* is the correct sentence.

3. is. The subject of the sentence is *picture,* which is singular, and not *wildflowers,* which is plural. The verb should agree with the subject, not the interrupting phrase. *The picture with wildflowers is my favorite* is the correct sentence.

4. quiet. The words *quiet* and *quite* have been confused.

Sally walked slowly through the quiet rooms is the correct sentence.

5. correct

6. correct

Working It Out
page 95

1. lose

2. quite

3. correct

4. to

5. correct

6. too

Here's an Example
page 96

Contractions:
were not → weren't
it is → it's

Working It Out
pages 96–97

1. They're not very friendly to anyone.

2. Who's making dinner tonight?

3. Its feathers are coming out.

4. Karen knows your mother quite well.

5. Jasper believes there's no reason to vote.

6. If you're not satisfied, let us know.

7. It's probably going to snow tonight.

8. Whose phone number is written in your notebook?

9. It's the number of my new neighbors. They're next door to me.

10. If it's theirs, tell me why there's a heart drawn around it!

Working It Out
pages 97–98

1. The Christmas trees, each crowned with a star, were beautiful.

2. George Kramer, like many other teachers, enjoys having the summer off.

3. This new cake mix with real walnuts is delicious.

4. Jacob and Frieda love to give gifts.

5. The day after final exams is the time to relax.

6. I, like my father, love a clean home.

7. My son and I don't agree about cleaning.

8. He, like all his friends, cleans house about once a year.

9. He and his friends say it just gets dirty again anyway.

Writing On Your Own
page 98

■ Some people say that patience is a virtue, but I think they're wrong. It's too easy to wait around until something good happens. I believe that life is your responsibility. Sometimes you, like everyone else, have to make things change. You can choose to do nothing or to take action. You won't win every time, but you will learn something even when you lose.

Part A / Lesson 27

Working It Out
page 101

Sample revision:
■ Drugs can save lives or take

lives. Drugs can help sick people get better, but they can also make people very sick. The difference depends on the way people use them.

Edited sentences:
■ The town of White River saw its first soccer match last Thursday. Our new soccer team, the White River Rockets, beat the Lincoln City Pirates. The score was 3–1.

Writing On Your Own
page 102

Here are some sample sentences that have been revised and edited.
My grandmother's house in Buffalo, New York, is one of my favorite places. My dad grew up in that large, comfortable house. Now my aunt and uncle, Sabina and Stefan, live there with their five children. My grandmother came from Poland, so we all speak Polish. We always sit in the kitchen and talk in Polish. We argue and laugh together. I always have a wonderful time.

Measuring What You've Learned
pages 103–106

Note: Some answers on Measuring What You've Learned are marked with an asterisk (*). This means there are many possible answers for that question. If you have an answer different from the one marked with an *, ask your teacher to tell you if your answer is also correct.

* **1.** Possible sentence: *The broken window is not important.* Your answer should replace the words *that's broke* and *no big deal* with more formal phrases.

2. The topic of this paragraph is *vegetables.*

3. *Keith may lose all his friends.* Since you could also say *Keith may have his friends taken away, lose* is the correct word choice.

4. *It's hard to cross the river right now.* Since you could rewrite the sentence as *It is hard to cross the river right now,* use the contraction form of *it,* or *it's.*

5. *I had quite a good time last night.* Since you could also say, *I had a very good time, quite* is the correct word choice.

6. *Your homework is missing.* Since the homework belongs to you, *your* is the correct word choice.

7. *Pleasant, pocket,* and *piece* would be on the dictionary page with the guide words *picture* and *poison.*

8. *Did Martha go to Arizona last winter?* The first letter in the sentence is capitalized. *Martha* and *Arizona* are capitalized because they are proper nouns. Since the sentence is a question, it ends with a question mark.

9. *Redbud Park opens for camping every May. Redbud Park* and *May* are capitalized because they are proper nouns. Since the sentence is a statement, it ends with a period.

10. *You shouldn't judge others without looking at yourself.* Since the pronouns *you* and *oneself* do not agree, one of them must be changed. *One shouldn't judge others without looking at oneself* is also correct.

11. *The puppy has its eyes open already.* Since there is only one puppy, to say *their* eyes is incorrect. *Its* eyes is correct. To say *his eyes* or *her eyes* would also be correct.

12. *We don't want to move. Don't* agrees with the subject, *we.*

13. *He is thinking about work all the time. Is* is the correct verb time for the sentence.

14. *The flowers were picked yesterday.* Since the action happened yesterday, the past verb time is correct. *Were* is in the past verb time.

15. *Larry saw a fight in the alley.* The verb *seen* cannot be used without a helping verb, so *saw* is the correct word choice.

16. *I hope John calls soon.* The verb *hope* agrees with the subject, *I.*

***17.** *Judy's boss told her the news.* The verb *was told* becomes the active verb *told.*

***18.** *The rabbit hopped through the bushes.* The verb *went* becomes the concrete verb *hopped.*

19. exclamation

20. command

21. question

22. Complete. The sentence has a dependent thought and an independent thought.

23. Fragment. The phrase does not have a complete, independent thought.

24. Comma splice. There are two independent thoughts joined only with a comma.

25. Complete. The subject is *time* and the verb is *flies.*

26. Run-on. The two independent thoughts are run together.

27. Run-on. The two independent thoughts are run together.

28. Milo was tired and hungry. You could also say, Milo was hungry and tired.

29. The large, powerful bear watched the deer.

30. *Jacques called me and talked about his girlfriend.* In this sentence the verbs have been combined.

31. *Alice and Vanessa believe in astrology.* In this sentence, the subjects have been combined.

32. *Melinda wants to buy a car, but she can't afford it.* Another correct sentence is: *She can't afford it, but Melinda wants to buy a car.*

33. *While we were on vacation, someone broke into our house.* Another correct sentence is: *Someone broke into our house while we were on vacation.*

34. *Don't park here, or you could get a ticket.*

35. *Even though Raissa loves pea soup, she won't eat peas.* You could also say: *Raissa loves pea soup even though she won't eat peas,* or *Even though she won't eat peas, Raissa loves pea soup.*

36. *World's busiest subway, A good way to travel,* and *Famous for its art* could be the three main topics. The other phrases could be given as subtopics or details under these main topics.

*37. Sample summary: *The Moscow subway, the busiest subway in the world, has many paintings and sculptures by top Russian artists. It is a good way to get around the city.*

38. It's not easy to learn another language. No matter where you're from, your own language always seems more simple than a language you don't know. Children often have fewer problems since they're able to copy many sounds. Whether the language is Spanish, Japanese, or Greek, children can often learn it faster than adults.

Part B / Lesson 1

Working It Out
pages 113–114

Purpose

1. describe
2. persuade
3. explain
4. tell about an event

Audience

1. cook
2. doctor
3. minister
4. teenager
5. driver
6. child
7. teacher
8. athlete
9. retired worker
10. mother

Smoking memo
Purpose: explain
Audience: smokers

Voting memo
Purpose: persuade
Audience: older voters

Writing On Your Own
page 114

Sample sentences:
Our town has a good semipro
hockey team.
It is only twenty miles from
a major league ball park.
This town has tennis courts
and a swimming pool.

Part B / Lesson 2

Working It Out
pages 116–117

Sample answers:

1. friendly, 25
2. brown, brown
3. 125
4. bright, flashy
5. go out and party
6. stay home and watch TV

Writing On Your Own
page 117

Sample answer:
I work in a gas station. Every
day I pump gas and work on
cars. I meet a lot of nice people. We talk and have fun. It is
a good job.

Part B / Lesson 3

Working It Out
page 120

Sample answers:

Prewriting: birthday party
for Bob   my house
small gift   8 P.M.
surprise   Friday, June 17

Writing: There's a birthday
party for my brother Bob. Your
invited. The party is a suprise.
It will be at my house on friday
June 17, at 8 P.M. We'll be give-
ing him just small, funny gifts

Revising: Your invited to a suprise party for my brother Bob.
It will be at my house on friday
June 17, at 8 P.M. We'll be give-
ing him small, funny gifts

Editing: ~~Your~~ *You're* invited to a
~~suprise~~ *surprise* party for my brother
Bob. It will be at my house
on ~~f~~*F*riday*,* June 17, at 8 P.M.
We'll be ~~giveing~~ *giving* him small,
funny gifts

Presenting: You're invited to a
surprise party for my brother
Bob. It will be at my house on
Friday, June 17, at 8 P.M. We'll
be giving him small, funny
gifts.

Writing On Your Own
page 120

Sample answers:

Prewriting: Topic—my hobby;
Ideas—collecting bottles
started when ten years old
50 bottles
uncle got me started
oldest is more than seventy

Writing: My hobby is collecting
bottles. Started when I was ten
years old. I now have fifty bottles, my oldest bottle is more
than seventy years old. My uncle got me started. Its fun to
collect these old bottles.

Revising: My hobby is collecting bottles. I started collecting
them when I was ten years old.
My Uncle Joe got me started. I
now have fifty bottles, my oldest bottle is more than seventy
years old. Its fun to collect
these old bottles.

Editing: My hobby is collecting bottles. I started collecting them when I was ten years old. My Uncle Joe got me started. I now have fifty bottles, ^M my oldest bottle is more ~~then~~ *than* seventy years old. It's fun to collect these old bottles.

Presenting: My hobby is collecting bottles. I started collecting them when I was ten years old. My Uncle Joe got me started. I now have fifty bottles. My oldest bottle is more than seventy years old. It's fun to collect these old bottles.

Part B / **Lesson 4**

Working It Out
page 122

Sample answers:

Person working in garden:

3. eat vegetables

4. water garden every day

Car lot:

3. small or big?

4. how many miles per gallon?

Writing On Your Own
page 123

Sample ideas:

new clothes	shopping mall
with friends	fun
groceries	market
record store	spend money

Sample sentences:

1. Going shopping at the mall is fun.

2. Shopping for groceries at the market is work.

3. My favorite place to spend money is the record store.

Part B / **Lesson 5**

Working It Out
pages 125–126

Reporter exercise

Who?	John Hays
What happened?	He was injured in a car accident.
When?	Friday night
Where?	on Main Street
Why?	The road was icy.
How?	He slid into a tree when he tried to turn the corner onto Maple Avenue.

Sample answers:

Who?	José, Emily, Derek, Carol, and I
What?	went to a concert
When?	last Saturday night
Where?	the Civic Center
Why?	The music was great and my friends are fun.
How . . .?	best time I've ever had! happy, excited

Writing On Your Own
page 126

Feel free to make up a story about the man and woman. Here are some sample answers.

Who?	a musician
What?	played the bongo
When?	on a hot summer day
Where?	in a park
Why?	for fun
How?	with a quick, rhythmic beat

Sentences:

1. The young musician played the bongo drum.

2. On a hot summer day, he played for fun.

3. The drumbeat sounded quick and rhythmic.

Part B / **Lesson 6**

Working It Out
pages 128–129

Topics
A. party actions
B. body parts
C. show love
D. expenses

Main idea
C. People can show their love in many different ways.
D. Daily life involves a lot of expenses.

Main ideas

1. Tom is a good friend in many ways.

2. People like all different kinds of music.

Writing On Your Own
page 129

Sample topic: uncle
Sample ideas:
there for me after Dad died
listened to me
spent time together
took me fishing
even yelled (when I needed it)
helped me buy first car
Sample main idea:
My uncle was a great help to
me after my father died.

Part B / Lesson 7

Working It Out
pages 131–132

1. Main Idea: A person can
   choose from many careers.
   Cross out—vacation, pay

2. Main Idea: I enjoy working
   outdoors.
   Cross out—pays less than
   an office job, Dad is an office worker

3. Main Idea: Watching TV
   can be good.
   Cross out—reading is better, boring

4. Cross Out—The streets are
   lined with stores.
   People who are sick need
   help too.

Writing On Your Own
page 132

Sample answers:
eat right
walk
go to doctor when sick
exercise in gym
~~sprained ankle once~~
don't eat junk food
keep weight down
get 8 hours' sleep each night
~~sometimes can't get to sleep~~

Main idea: There are many
things I do to keep healthy.

Part B / Lesson 8

Working It Out
pages 134–135

Sunday, June 11
rain dates—June 17 and 18
Place
green house with black
    shutters
bikes
clothing

Writing On Your Own
page 135

Sample answer:

What I do each week

1. Weekdays
   go to part-time job
   go to night school
   do housework
   bowl Thursday nights

2. Weekends
   buy groceries
   work in yard
   go out with friends

Part B / Lesson 9

Working It Out
pages 137–138

Sample answers:

Jobs around the House

1. vacuum

2. do dishes

3. wash clothes

4. dust

5. take out garbage

Clothes to Bring

1. sweaters

2. Winter

3. boots

4. gloves

5. Summer

6. swimsuit

7. T-shirt

Writing On Your Own
page 138

Sample map: See Fig. C.

Part B / Lesson 10

Working It Out
pages 141–142

A.
Sherman is a clever basketball
player.
My company is made up of
three parts.
Finding a husband is a hard
task.

Figure C: Word map for Part B, Lesson 9, page 138

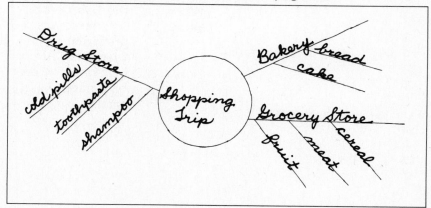

B.

1. C. Games are a popular way to spend free time.

2. B. There is going to be a birthday party.

Writing On Your Own
page 142

Sample topic sentence:
The people in my family like different shows on TV.

Sample paragraph:
The show I like best on TV is "Jeopardy." The host reads answers to the three people on the show. The people earn money for each right question they ask. It is exciting to see who will win. But, most of all, I learn many things from hearing the questions and answers.

Part B / Lesson 11

Working It Out
pages 144—145

A. Sample details:

1. Some people like horror movies that scare them.

2. Many people like romantic love stories.

3. There are the funny comedy movies to make you laugh.

4. Adventure movies with chases and spies are fun.

B. Sample paragraph:
Traffic lights give important directions. They tell drivers what to do at crossroads. The red light on top tells drivers to stop. The yellow light in the middle means that the light is changing. The driver should be careful before moving ahead. The green light on the bottom tells drivers to go ahead. Traffic lights prevent many accidents.

Writing On Your Own
page 145

Sample details:

1. cars, buses, taxis

2. planes

3. ships, boats

4. walking

Sample paragraph:
There are many means of transportation that people can use today. On land, they can drive or ride in cars, buses, and taxis. If they need to go far, they can fly in a plane. To go across water, they ride on a boat or a big ship. When they need to go just a little way, they can walk there. There's a means of transportation for everyone.

Part B / Lesson 12

Working It Out
pages 147—148

1. lie on the beach or swim

2. see a baseball game

3. the Old State House and the Old North Church

4. the site of the Battle of Bunker Hill

Writing On Your Own
page 148

Sample answers:
You will feel better.

1. You won't get tired so fast.

2. You will be able to breathe more deeply and easily.

You will look better.

3. You won't have a cigarette dangling from your mouth all the time.

4. You won't have stains on your teeth or fingers.

Sample paragraph:
You really should quit smoking. For one thing, you will feel better. If you quit, you won't get tired so fast. You will be able to breathe more deeply and easily. You will also look better. You won't have a cigarette dangling from your mouth all the time. You won't have stains from tobacco on your teeth and fingers either. Think how much healthier and happier you'll be.

Part B / Lesson 13

Working It Out
pages 150—151

A. 5, 6, 3, 1, 4, 2
B. 4, 1, 3, 2
C. Sample answers:

2. Lisa felt depressed.

3. You go to bed.

4. You pass the test.

Writing On Your Own
page 151

A. Sample paragraph:
Writing a paragraph is not too hard. First, you think of ideas to write about. Next, you find a main idea and details to tell about the main idea. Then you make an outline or map to organize your ideas. Now you are ready to start writing the paragraph.

B. Sample paragraph:
Different kinds of weather have different effects on me. Blue skies and sunshine make me cheerful, of course. Gray skies and chilly temperatures can bring me down. However, a good old thunderstorm excites me. On the other hand, a quiet snowstorm makes me feel thoughtful and peaceful.

Part B / Lesson 14

Working It Out
pages 153–154

A. 1, 3, 5, 2, 4
B. Sample answers:
3, 4, 1, 2, 6, 5, 7
or 6, 2, 1, 3, 4, 5, 7
There are different ways to order the details in a paragraph like this. You can go back and forth from city to country. Or you can tell all about the city first and then about the country.

Writing On Your Own
page 154

A. Sample paragraph:
People need to be able to read. First, reading helps you know about life around you, like the news of your city and the world. Reading helps you do your job better. It lets you read labels on foods, so you're a better shopper. Last, reading can be fun.

B. Sample paragraph:
My home and my brother's home are very different. I live in a big apartment building with twenty floors. My brother Sam lives in a little one-family house with one floor. My home is red brick. His home is white with green trim. I live in the middle of a big city. Sam lives in a small town.

Part B / Lesson 15

Working It Out
page 158

1. Yes. Two dead trees on State Street should be cut down.

2. Details: The trees don't look very nice. They might fall and kill or hurt someone. They might be blown down on a house. Yes, they all support the main idea.

3. There's nothing to explain the first detail. You could add something like, "They hurt the appearance of a lovely street" or "They make it seem as if the city doesn't care about its streets." The other two details are explained by facts. The trees might kill or hurt someone *because* people are often on the street. Also, the trees might hit a house *because* two houses are near each tree.

4. Sample answer: Yes. The detail about the look of the trees is not too important. It's much less important than people being hurt or killed. It's less important than houses being damaged. The detail would be better at the end of the paragraph.

Writing On Your Own
page 158

Sample paragraph:
My sister, Coretta, and I are very different. She has short, curly black hair, and I have long, wavy black hair. She is tall, but I am just five feet tall. Coretta loves to play sports and to jog. I'd rather read a book or watch TV. She and I are not very much alike at all.

Part B / Lesson 16

Working It Out
page 161

A. Sample answers:

1. Then (or Second, or Next)

2. Therefore, (or Consequently,)

3. On the other hand, (or But or However,)

4. Likewise, (or Similarly,)

5. As a result, (or Therefore, or For that reason,)

B. Sample answers:
First
Next
Then
Finally
In conclusion

Writing On Your Own
page 161

Sample paragraph:
On Tuesday, I came down with the flu. For that reason, I stayed home from work. Since I felt awful, I looked for some medicine such as aspirin and cough syrup. By then I had a high fever. Therefore, I decided to call the doctor.

Part B / Lesson 17

Working It Out
pages 163–164

A. Sample answers:

1. Because Jim ate too much pizza, he became very sick.

2. Once she focused her camera, she took our picture.

B. Sample answers:

1. What is the best kind of dog to have?

2. Teach your dog to obey you.

3. That dog is the funniest-looking animal I've ever seen!

C. Sample answers:

1. By the time the game began, Joe was tired.

2. Slowly, Mr. Kane repeated the words.

Writing On Your Own
page 164

Sample paragraph:
Do you like basketball? It is my favorite sport. When I was five or six, I started playing basketball on the playground. Trying to get the ball in that little basket was fun. I loved the game. Even today, it is the game I like to play in my free time.

Part B / Lesson 18

Working It Out
page 167

A. Sample answers:

1. tornado, snowstorm, hurricane

2. fry, boil, bake

3. nibble, chew, gulp

B.

1. The huge fish weighed more than 100 pounds.

2. The party began at 8 P.M.

Writing On Your Own
page 167

A. Sample revised paragraph: We like to have parties at the state park. It is a beautiful place. Everyone has a relaxing time. We gulp down lots of soda and nibble away at huge amounts of good chicken wings. People play softball and listen to rock music. It is always fun.

B. Sample revised paragraph: People who have twins have a hard job. They have twice the work. Parents of baby twins are just beginning years of taking care of two children who are alike.

Part B / Lesson 19

Working It Out
page 170

A.

1. She was reading the *Los Angeles Times* of Friday, July 1.

2. Her father, **Mr.** Koros, works for **Hart Paper Company**.

3. George's uncle fought in the Vietnam **War**.

B.

1. She worked for Mr. T. J. Orso in Kent, Ohio, until May 1, 1988.

2. Nikki took her coat, her purse, and her keys with her.

3. After we put up the tent for the boys, it rained.

C.

1. counties   2. correct

3. correct   4. monkeys

5. loving   6. hopeful

D.

1. Maurita **comes** to see her father every day.

2. As the sun **set**, we walked back to camp.

3. The store sold out all **its** sale items.

Part B / Lesson 20

Working It Out
pages 171–172

A.

1. Miss Esther L. Lee was born on **February 20, 1968**.

2. Lake Huron is **perhaps** the most **beautiful** of the Great Lakes.

3. I am **hoping** that we will see our friends **there**.

4. Four silly, giggling toddlers **were** playing in the yard.

5. Dr. Hosbach **went** to the hospital in a hurry.

B.

You often read only about bad people in the news. However, there are many good people in our town. Mr Janski is the mayor. He works for the scott book company [S B C] and has his dutys [duties] as mayor too. Dr parks [P] take [s] care of the sick men, women, and children in town. The doctor is respected by all who know her. Mrs. Osgood is the principle [principal] of the school. She is a good freind [friend] to the children their. [There] Our town, Waterford, Alabama, is a place full of good people.

Writing On Your Own
page 172

Sample paragraph:
I've lived twenty-five years, and I've learned which things are truly important. My house is important to me. My husband and I worked very hard to be able to buy it. My health is important too. Without good health, it's hard to enjoy life. Most important of all is my family. My husband and my two beautiful children mean more to me than anything else possibly could.

GED Challenger
page 173

1. (5) The word *compeny* should be spelled *company.* It should not be capitalized, though. It is not part of the name of a specific company in the sentence.

2. (4) Both *Mrs.* and *Jones* should be capitalized.

3. (1) The first word of a sentence is always capitalized.

Part B / Lesson 21

Working It Out
page 175

You may have decided to change some things the woman wrote. Then you should have written the paragraph neatly in the space provided.

Writing On Your Own
page 176

Your paragraph should have a clear message, be written well, have no errors, and be written neatly in the space provided.

Part B / Lesson 22

Working It Out
pages 179–180

You should copy the story just the way it is printed.

Writing On Your Own
page 180

Sample paragraph:
Yesterday, everything was great! I wanted to go shopping. When I started to get into my car, I found some money. It was a ten-dollar bill just lying on the ground with no wallet around. Then I started to drive down the street. I saw an old friend crossing the street. I hadn't seen him in two years. I stopped and we had a nice, long chat. I was glad I had gone out in my car.

Part B / Lesson 23

Working It Out
pages 182–183

Main idea: Jim's return home was happy.

1. Trip to the airport
whole family left early
excited on the way out

2. Jim arrived
hugs and kisses all around
so happy we cried
took a family picture

Writing On Your Own
page 183

Sample ideas:
the story "The Most Dangerous Game"
man hunts man   tricks
island   scary   tiger pit
jumps off cliff
knife   jungle

Sample questions:
Who?   General Zaroff and Rainsford
What?   hunt
When?   night
Where?   jungle on Shiptrap Island
Why?   Zaroff bored with hunting
How?   chase through jungle

Sample idea: One man chases another man in a hunt in the jungle.

Sample outline:
1. Zaroff hunts Rainsford
Zaroff bored with hunting
jungle island—Shiptrap Island
night
2. Rainsford uses tricks
tiger pit
knife slingshot
3. Rainsford escapes
jumps off cliff
kills Zaroff

Part B / Lesson 24

Working It Out
page 185

Sample topic sentence: It was certainly a happy day when my son Jim returned home.

Sample paragraph completion: everyone gave him hugs and kisses. We all cried because we were so happy. Uncle Joe took a family picture of us so that we could remember that happy day.

Writing On Your Own
page 186

Sample first draft:
An exciting story I read is about a chase in the jungle. The story starts out on Shiptrap Island at night. General Zaroff is bored with hunting animals. He decides to hunt a man named Rainsford. Rainsford runs into the jungle to escape. Rainsford builds a tiger pit. Zaroff's dog falls into it. Rainsford makes a slingshot with a branch and his knife. It hits Zaroff's servant. Zaroff is about to catch Rainsford. Rainsford jumps off a cliff into the ocean. But he doesn't die. He sneaks back to Zaroff's house and kills him.

Part B / Lesson 25

Working It Out
page 189

Sample revised and edited paragraph:

I got up ~~erly~~ *early* and put on my best suit. ~~This was~~ *L*ast Friday, ~~which~~ was a very good day for me. *Then* I drove to the Beekman Printing *C*company. I went to see Mr. J K Beekman in his office. He talked to me about a new job opening. I told him that I could run a press and manage people. He like*d* what I had to say. ~~about~~ ~~what I could do.~~ *In fact,* Mr. Beekman offered me a job. What a *great* ~~grate~~ day it turned out to be!

Writing On Your Own
page 189

Make sure you've checked off all the points on the Revising Checklist and on the Editing Checklist. After all your work, be sure your narrative is neat enough for someone to read it.

Sample finished narrative paragraph:
An exciting story I read is about a deadly chase in the jungle. The story starts on Shiptrap Island at night. General Zaroff is bored with hunting animals. He decides to hunt a man named Rainsford instead. Rainsford runs into the jungle to escape. First, Rainsford builds a tiger pit. Zaroff's dog falls into it. Then, Rainsford makes a slingshot with a branch and his knife. It hits Zaroff's servant. When Zaroff is about to catch Rainsford, Rainsford jumps off a cliff into the ocean. But he doesn't die. He sneaks back to Zaroff's house and kills him at the end of the story.

Part B / Lesson 26

Working It Out
pages 191–192

You should copy the paragraph just the way it is printed.

Writing On Your Own
page 192

Sample paragraph:
Jack's garage is the place where I work. It is a dirty, white wood building on First Street. The big sign in front says, "We can fix anything you can drive." In front of the garage are five or six old cars that are used for parts. You always hear the sound of hammers there. You smell oil and dust when you go into the garage. It is a messy place, but a good place to work.

Part B / Lesson 27

Working It Out
pages 194–195

Sample main idea: My baby has different moods.

Sample outline:
When she's happy
 1. Looks
    pinkish glow
    smiles
    blue eyes light up
 2. Sounds
    coos
    hums
 3. Feels
    cuddly
When she's sad or mad
 1. Looks
    reddish
    teary cheeks
    puffed cheeks
 2. Sounds
    sobs
    shrill cry
 3. Feels
    wiggly

Writing On Your Own
page 195

Sample answers:
Looks—brown, curly hair, green eyes, tall, slim, jeans
Smells—clean, like soap; sometimes nice cologne
Sounds—deep voice, loud
Feels—rough skin, wiry hair

Sample main idea: My husband is a handsome man.

Sample outline:
 1. Looks
    brown curly hair
    green eyes
    tall
    slim
 2. Smells
    clean, like soap
    cologne—nice
 3. Sounds
    deep voice
    loud
 4. Feels
    wiry hair
    rough skin

Part B / Lesson 28

Working It Out
pages 197–198

Sample topic sentence: Like a grown-up, my baby has different moods.

Sample paragraph completion: her face turns reddish and sour.

Tears wet her puffed cheeks. Her little sobs can break your heart. Those sobs may turn into a long, shrill cry. Then she becomes so wiggly. But I love her no matter what mood she's in.

Writing On Your Own
page 198

Sample first draft:
My husband, Paul, is a handsome man. Paul is tall and slim. He has brown, curly hair and green eyes. His hair feels wiry. He always smells clean, like soap. I love the smell of the pine-smelling cologne on his rough skin. Paul has a loud, deep voice that can be heard all around. He is a good-looking man.

Part B / Lesson 29

Working It Out
page 201

Sample revised and edited paragraph:

Standing on the corner of Broad Street and Third Avenue is intresting. People in heavy winter coats, scarves, and gloves rush by. Some People bump into each other and mumble "Excuse me" or "Sorry." Big blue buses stop, and more People pile out. Bus fumes fill the air. A shiny silver pretzel cart is there. A man in a blue snowsuit stands beside it. The salty, yeasty smell of pretzels goes through the air. The

hum of car and bus engines and the honking of horns are loud at this busy spot

Writing On Your Own
page 201

Sample finished descriptive paragraph:
My husband, Paul, is a handsome man. Paul is tall, slim, and well built. He has brown, curly hair and striking green eyes. He always smells clean, like soap. I also love the smell of his pine-scented cologne and the feel of his rough skin. That roughness comes from hard work outdoors. Paul has a loud, deep voice that can be heard all around. He is a good-looking man.

Part B / Lesson 30

Working It Out
page 205

You should copy the paragraph just the way it is printed.

Writing On Your Own
page 206

Sample paragraph:
Getting from my house to the

beach is not hard. First, you walk east to the corner of Pine and Elm Streets. There you get on the D bus. Ride north on the bus until you get to Tenth Street. Get off the bus there. You will be in front of the public library. Walk two blocks east down Tenth Street, and you will be at the beach.

Part B / Lesson 31

Working It Out
pages 208–209

Sample main idea: There are certain things to look for in a job.

Sample map: see Fig. D below.

Writing On Your Own
page 209

Sample answers:
Brainstorming:

hiking	exercise
talk	keep slim
fresh air	see people
healthy	see trees, flowers

Questions:
Who: anyone can—old and young, alone or with another
What: hiking

Figure D: Word map for Part B, Lesson 31, page 209

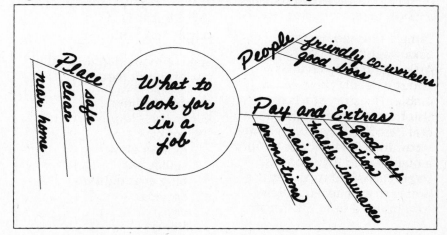

When: all day, evening, any
season
Where: paths, fields, parks, in
the country
Why: healthy exercise,
relaxing
How: just move your feet

Main idea: Hiking is a good
activity.

Hiking is good for you.
1. Healthy
good exercise
keep slim
breathe fresh air
relaxing
2. Meet people
talk
3. See nature
trees
flowers

Part B / Lesson 32

Working It Out
pages 211–212

Sample topic sentence:
There are certain things you
should look for in a job.

Sample paragraph completion:
You want the place to be safe
and clean. A company near
your home will save you time
and money. Last, you want a
good boss and friendly people
to work with.

Writing On Your Own
page 212

Sample first draft:
Hiking is a great activity that
makes you feel good. It helps
you stay healthy. The good exercise keeps you slim. When
you hike, you breathe fresh air.
That is good for your lungs and
body. Hiking also relaxes you.
Another good thing about hiking is that it helps you meet
and talk with other people. It

also gets you outside to enjoy
the pretty trees and flowers in
nature.

Part B / Lesson 33

Working It Out
page 214

Sample revised and edited
paragraph:

Playing cards is something my
friends and ~~me~~ _I_ like to do. _In fact,_ Joe
Jane, Bill Madsen, Pete Judge
and I play cards every ~~F~~riday
night. It's a ~~good~~ _relaxing_ way to spend
free time. ~~It's relaxing.~~ We
laugh and try to ~~beet~~ _beat_ each
other at the game. It is also a
unique ~~good~~ way to make ~~your mind~~ _our minds_
work. ~~We~~ _For example,_ try to ~~figure a way~~ _think of_ _5_ to
win. We try to figure out the
cards the other players ~~has~~ _have_ in
their hands. Playing cards is ~~a~~ _an excellent_
~~good way~~ _and enjoyable reason_ to get together.

Writing On Your Own
page 215

Sample finished explanatory
paragraph:
Hiking is a great activity for
making you feel good. For one
thing, hiking helps you stay
healthy. This easy exercise
keeps you slim. When you hike,
you breathe fresh air, not stale
indoor air. Fresh air helps your
lungs, your heart, and the rest
of your body. Second, hiking
relaxes you. You can enjoy and
feel a part of the majestic
trees, flowers, and animals of
nature. Finally, hiking can improve your social activity, even
if you are alone! When you
hike, you often meet and talk

with other hikers. Who can re-
sist such a rewarding activity?

GED Challenger
page 215

Sample answer:
People like to watch TV for
many reasons. Some people
learn from TV. They watch the
news to discover what is going
on in the world. Children learn
their ABCs and other skills
from TV too. Other people
watch TV to relax. When you
sit down and watch TV, you
don't have to work. You just
loaf. The TV does all the work.
It tells you a story or makes you
laugh.

Part B / Lesson 34

Working It Out
pages 217–218

You should copy the paragraph
just the way it is printed.

Writing On Your Own
page 218

Sample answer:
Eating right will help you in
many ways. If you eat foods
from the main food groups
each day, you will look and feel
better. Your skin will look
smoother. It will also have
more color. Your shape will be
slimmer too. You will have
more energy and feel you can
do almost anything. So start
eating right. You'll be glad you
did.

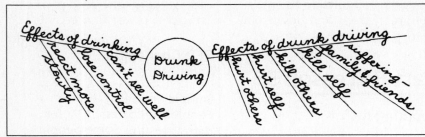

Figure E: Word map for Part B, Lesson 35, page 221

Part B / **Lesson 35**

Working It Out
page 221

Sample main idea: Don't drink and drive.

Sample map: see Figure E, above.

Writing On Your Own
page 221

Sample answers:
Brainstorm:

neat	work hard
careful	friendly
on time	can do word
	processing
can file	need money
look nice	trusted

Questions:
Who: me
What: can do word processing and filing

When: can start now, can work long hours and overtime
Where: can drive anywhere in city
Why: need to earn money, want to work for a good company
How: will do a good job

Main idea: You should hire me.

Sample map: see Figure F, below.

Part B / **Lesson 36**

Working It Out
pages 223–224

Sample paragraph completion: You could kill yourself or somebody else. You could cripple yourself or other people. Also, your family and friends would suffer if you or someone else was killed or hurt.

Figure F: Word map for Part B, Lesson 35, page 221

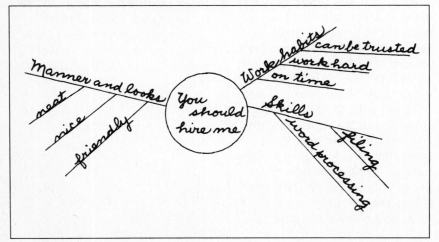

Writing On Your Own
page 224

Sample first draft:
You should hire me for many reasons. Most important, I work very hard on a job. I can be trusted to do a good job and to get it done on time. I can file and do word processing. Both of these things I did on my last job. I also look nice on the job. I wear neat clothes, and I am always friendly to other people. For these reasons, you should hire me for this job.

Part B / **Lesson 37**

Working It Out
pages 226–227

Sample revised and edited paragraph:

You should come to work

with us in the family bakery.
 comfortable right
You could make a living here.
from the beginning.
You'll earn good money and
 future
get raises in the ~~futur~~.
 even
Someday you will become
 Many people never get such a chance.
your own boss. Also, you'll be
 build
helping ~~bild~~ our family's name

in the neighborhood. *You'll be*

Carrying on a family tradition.

It would make your mother
 so pleased and proud I
and me ~~feel good~~ .think

about coming to work with

us.

Writing On Your Own
page 227

Sample finished persuasive paragraph:
I can offer you several solid reasons for hiring me. Most im-

portant, I work hard on a job. I can be trusted to do a good job and to get it done on time. My special skills are word processing and filing, but I'm a good learner too. In addition, I am professional on the job. I have a neat appearance and am always friendly to co-workers and customers. If you want a hard-working employee, hire me for the job.

Part B / Lesson 38

Working It Out
page 229

Sample answers:
I like Christmas because it is a time to celebrate my religious beliefs.
I also like the 4th of July because we have a huge picnic outside.

Holiday 1   Christmas
family gets together
big turkey dinner
fun to give and get gifts
Holiday 2   4th of July
family gets together
sunny and warm outside
see fireworks

Writing On Your Own
page 230

Sample letter:
   I have two favorite holidays. The special days I enjoy the most are Christmas and the 4th of July.
   I like Christmas because it is a time to celebrate my religious beliefs. They are very important to me. Also important is my family. Christmas is a time when we all get together. We have a big turkey dinner with all the trimmings. It's fun to get Christmas presents too.

It's even more fun to give them. Perhaps the most fun of all is watching the children open theirs.
   I also like the 4th of July because we have a huge picnic outside. Just like Christmas, the whole family is there. The weather is usually beautiful too—sunny and warm. The holiday is a good excuse to sit outside and relax. Even the night is usually warm, so we all walk to the park and watch the wonderful fireworks.
   I like other holidays too, but Christmas and the 4th of July are my favorites.

Part B / Lesson 39

Working It Out
pages 232–233

Sample paragraph:
Why are fast-food restaurants popular? They serve food fast when you are in a hurry. You always know what kind of food you will get. These restaurants are convenient. They are also places where you can buy food for a small price. These are some of the reasons fast-food restaurants are popular.

Writing On Your Own
page 233

Sample outline:
Main idea: Fast food restaurants are popular.

1. They serve food fast when you are in a hurry.
   get food in less than 5 minutes
   breakfast on the way to work
   a quick lunch so you can shop on lunch hour

2. You always know what kind of food you will get.
   same things on menu all the time
   same taste every time you go—no surprises

3. These restaurants are convenient.
   near main highways
   in shopping areas
   near tourist places

4. They are also places where you can buy food for a small price.
   buy single items
   lunch for less than $2.00
   coupons

Index

Agreement
  pronouns and nouns, 39–41
  subject and verb, 42–45, 73,
    97–98, 170
Audience, 9–10, 112, 113–14

Brainstorming, 121–23, 126, 129,
  130, 207, 221

Capitalization, 34–37, 54–56,
  168–69, 170, 171–72
Cause and effect, 77, 149–51, 152,
  160, 205, 206
Combining complete thoughts, 76–78
Combining sentences, 72–75, 97
Combining unequal ideas, 79–82
Comma, 17, 169
  for combining sentences and
    complete thoughts, 73, 74, 76,
    77
  with dependent thoughts, 64, 80
  with descriptive details, 66, 67
  with descriptive phrases, 70
Commands, 57–59, 162, 163, 164
Comma splice, 63, 64–65
Comparisons and contrasts, 152–54,
  160, 197, 198
Concise words, 165–67
Connecting words
  for combining complete thoughts,
    76, 77–78
  for combining sentences, 73–75
  dependent thoughts and, 80, 81
  descriptive details and, 66–67
  run-on sentences and, 64
Context clues, 21–23, 48
Contractions, 94, 96–97

Dependent thoughts, 64, 80–82
Descriptive details, 31–33, 66–68,
  116–17
Descriptive phrases, 69–71
Descriptive writing, 190–201
Dictionary, 25–26, 169

Editing, 99, 100–102, 119, 120,
  168–73
  checklists for, 100, 171, 188, 200,
    214, 226
  descriptive writing, 199–201
  explanatory writing, 213–15
  narrative writing, 187–89
  persuasive writing, 225–27
Essay writing, 231–33
  for GED, 215
Exclamation points, 17, 54, 55, 58
Exclamations, 57–59, 162, 163, 164
Explanatory writing, 204–15

Final copies, presenting, 119, 120,
  174–76, 201
First draft, 119, 140, 143, 159
  of descriptive writing, 196–98

of explanatory writing, 210–12
of narrative writing, 184–86
of persuasive writing, 222–24
Free writing, 18–20

GED Test, 122, 173, 215
  Spelling List, 22
  Writing Test, 65
Grammar, 170, 171–72
Guide words, 25, 26

Handwriting, 14–17, 175, 176

Independent thoughts, 60, 79–82
Interrupting phrases, 94, 97–98

Journal, 16, 20, 25, 27, 41, 62

Linking words, 159–61, 211

Main idea(s), 79, 127–29, 231. See
  also Supporting details; Topic
  sentence in an essay, 231, 233
  in more than one paragraph,
    228, 229, 230
Mapping ideas, 136–38

Narrative writing, 178–89
Note-taking, 83–86
Nouns, 34–37

Order of importance, 152–54, 160,
  217, 224
Outlining, 87–90, 133–35, 136, 138

Paragraphs, 115–17
  ending, 160
  organization of, 231
  writing more than one, 228–30
Period, 17, 54–56, 64, 169
Persuasive writing, 216–27
Possessives, 94, 96–97
Prewriting, 118, 119, 120, 123, 136.
  See also Brainstorming;
    Mapping ideas; Outlining;
    Questions for writing ideas
  Descriptive writing, 193–95
  explanatory writing, 207–9
narrative writing, 181–83
  persuasive writing, 291–21
Pronouns, 38–41, 170
  possessive, 96
Proper nouns, 34–37
Punctuation, 17, 169, 171–72
Purpose for writing, 9–10, 112–14,
  115–16, 117

Question mark, 54, 55, 58
Questions, 57–59, 162, 163, 164
Questions for writing ideas, 124–26,
  207, 221

Revising, 99–102, 118, 119, 120,
  156–58, 165, 166, 167
  checklists for, 99, 156, 187–88,
    200, 214, 226
  descriptive writing, 199–201

explanatory writing, 213–15
narrative writing, 187–89
persuasive writing, 225–27
Run-on sentences, 63–65

Semicolon, 64
Sense words, 32–33, 190–92
Sentence fragments, 61–62
Sentences
  beginning and ending, 54–56, 168
  complete, 60–62
  tying together, 159–61
  types of, 57–59
  using a variety of, 162–64
Space order, 197, 198
Specific words, 190–92
Spelling, 169, 171–72
Statements, 57–59, 162, 163, 164
  punctuation for, 169
Step-by-step order, 205, 206
Subjects, 42–45, 59, 60
  combining, 73, 74–75, 97
Summarizing, 91–93
Supporting details, 143–45, 231
  developing, 146–48
  relating, 149–54
  selecting, 130–32

Thesaurus, 33
Time order, 149–51, 152, 160, 184,
  186, 205
Topic, 11–13, 127–28, 129
  details and, 31
Topic sentence, 149–42, 145, 228,
  231, 232

Verbs, 42–45, 60, 97–98
  active, 50–52
  combining, 74–75
  concrete, 50–52
  helping, 47
  irregular, 45, 48
  regular, 47
Verb time, 46–49, 170
Vocabulary, 24–25, 27

Word bank, 25, 27
Word choice, 165–67
Word endings, 169
Word lists, 28–30, 33, 52
Word maps, 28, 29, 30
Words, new
  finding, 24–27
  grouping, 28–30
  learning, 21–23
Word sets, confusing, 94, 95
Writing, 8–10, 121–26. See also
    Descriptive writing; Explanatory
    writing; Narrative writing;
    Persuasive writing
  fine-tuning, 94–98
Writing process, 118–20. See also
    Editing; First Draft; Prewriting;
    Revising
Writing Skills, survey of, 2–5, 103–6,
  108–9, 234–36